THE EXPANDING CIRCLE

Marion F. Wolff

MARION FREYER WOLFF

THE EXPANDING CIRCLE

An Adoption Odyssey

FITHIAN PRESS, SANTA BARBARA, CALIFORNIA, 2000

Published by Fithian Press
A division of Daniel and Daniel, Publishers, Inc.
Post Office Box 1525
Santa Barbara, CA 93102

LIBRARY OF CONGRESS CATALOGING-IN-PUBLICATION DATA
Wolff, Marion Freyer.
   The expanding circle : an adoption odyssey / by Marion Freyer Wolff.
        p.   cm.
   ISBN 1-56474-318-7 (alk. paper)
   1. Intercountry adoption.   2. Jews, American—Germany (West)   3. Holocaust
survivors—Germany (West)   I. Title.
HV875.5.W65   2000
362.73'4—dc21   99-30768
                                                                     CIP

In memory of my uncle and aunt,
Erwin and Lotte Lichtenstein,
whose encouragement played an important part
in our adoption odyssey.

Preface

In writing this book I relied on the factual information contained in the diaries that my husband, John, and I kept from August 9 to November 6, 1958. My parents-in-law saved many letters and cards we had sent them from Europe. This correspondence recorded not only our itinerary but also our anxieties and emotional ups and downs, and helped recreate many details of our search.

In order to protect the privacy of the people we encountered, the names of many individuals and some places have been changed. I am grateful that Miss Ilse Heins, director of the orphanage, gave me written permission to use her name. Mrs. Ursula Tremel, widow of Judge Kurt Tremel, graciously consented to my using her late husband's name.

I have taken the liberty of inventing the wording of many dialogues while taking great care to preserve the speakers' personalities and characters. Photographs and 8-millimeter home movies helped me recall the faces of people and the features of the landscape.

Historical information is based on extensive research. I have listed my sources at the end of the book. My husband, John, was my most valuable resource. When we spent many hours comparing the entries of our diaries and reminiscing, we were quite amazed to discover how many minute details of our adventure we actually remembered. Our daughter, Rebecca, encouraged me by asking important questions concerning the why and how of her adoption.

Thanks go to John for typing the original manuscript; to two good friends, Rena Cohen Kelly and Francis McGuire, who read the first draft and offered valuable criticism; and to Joshua Orenstein, who typed the revised manuscript. But most of all I thank Rebecca, for without her there would have been no story to tell. By expanding our circle, she helped change three lives forever.

THE EXPANDING CIRCLE

I

After a three-year wait we decided to take matters into our own hands. It was 1957, and according to the rules of the agency handling adoptions, women who had reached the age of thirty-three were considered too old to become adoptive mothers. The waiting lists were endless, and a three-year wait was not unusual. Many couples resorted to the "gray market" to avoid the bureaucratic hurdles, but we had decided against that.

I was going to be thirty-three in the summer of 1958, and even though we had met every possible qualification and presumably were near the top of the waiting list, there was no guarantee if and when a child would be assigned to us. I was beginning to envy my friends, who could expect a nine-month pregnancy, while I had to endure year after year of an uncertain waiting period.

A friend suggested we try our luck in Europe. After all, John and I had been born in Europe and thought we could easily find our way around the maze of affidavits, questionnaires, letters of reference, and other elements of the "*Papierkrieg*" (paper war) that we would have to wage. On the other hand, I had grave doubts about returning to the place where the "Final Solution of the Jewish problem" had almost become a reality. Under no circumstances would we be able to return to Berlin, our birthplace. The memories of the Nazi years were still painfully vivid.

Luckily, the Fourth International Congress of Biochemistry was to take place in Vienna September 1 through 6, 1958. Perhaps we could combine our search with attendance at the congress. Moreover, John was to begin his new work as a biochemist at the National Institutes of Health in mid-November, and I had already made arrangements to leave my teaching position at the end of the 1957–58 school year. We decided to allow about twelve weeks for our trip. It was relatively easy to fix the endpoints of our adventure: departure on the M.S.

Kungsholm from New York City on Saturday, August 9, and return on the M.S. *Gripsholm* from Bremerhaven on October 29, scheduled arrival in New York on Thursday, November 6, 1958, leaving about ten weeks for the actual search.

As we began to prepare for our quest, we soon realized that we would need the help of a wide network of supporters to carry out our plan within the time limits we had set. After contacting the consulates of many European countries we learned that Germany was, indeed, the only country that permitted the release of any children for overseas adoption. Every other country, if not forbidding foreign adoptions outright, had many restrictions concerning religion and citizenship that immediately disqualified us. Therefore, we needed to concentrate our search in Germany and we were looking for friends who could provide advice and, possibly, leads, to help us set up an itinerary in what was then West Germany.

It had been less than nineteen years since we fled Germany as stateless refugees, and we still spoke German fluently. We even remembered the pre-Hitler culture: As children we had recited poems by Goethe, Schiller, and Heine and had sung the lovely folksongs as we hiked in the countryside. As teenagers we had studied the lyrical art songs of Schubert and Brahms, and even staged an abbreviated version of Mozart's *The Magic Flute*.

The dark cloud that descended on Germany in 1933 effectively ended any creative expression. As all the great minds were forced to flee or be silenced forever, this "civilized" country sank into a state of barbarism last witnessed in the Middle Ages. Could we dare hope in 1958 that the dark cloud had lifted sufficiently for us to return to this land and walk about without fear? Of course, we could not forget. And we were not entitled to forgive. Only the dead could do that. There were many questions that we needed to resolve before we could attempt to adopt a "German" child.

Is there such an entity as a "German" child? Does the place where one happens to come into this world determine the character or development of a human being? According to our religion there is no "original sin." Every baby is pure and innocent, a unique individual, endowed with the ability to choose between good and evil. Children are not responsible for the sins of their fathers. They are entitled to live in the present and the future and be judged on their own merits.

These were the beliefs that justified our return to Germany in search of a child. We realized that our ideas were in direct opposition to the racial theories that had been advanced by the Nazis and enthusiastically embraced by the great majority of German physicians and scientists. As we were to discover later, the old prejudices and superstitions, plus the genetic theories propagated by the Nazis, were deeply ingrained in the German psyche. They were to play a significant role in our search.

Saturday, August 9 was a perfect day. John's family had accompanied us to the pier. We had boarded the M.S. *Kungsholm* at 9 A.M. As we stood on the deck and waved to the crowd below, a great sense of accomplishment came over us. Here we were, ready to begin our great adventure! This pier on 57th Street was the springboard into the unknown.

The boat was to leave at 11 A.M., and we decided to inspect our stateroom and make sure that our luggage had been delivered to the right cabin. The tiny air-conditioned space that was to be our home for nine days was tastefully furnished. We could see the sun dancing on the water outside our very own porthole, and there was even a shower in the bathroom. We were thinking of how this luxury contrasted with the squalid conditions of the overcrowded refugee ships that had cautiously made their way across the ocean during wartime. I remembered the minesweepers that had accompanied our boat and the huge warships on the horizon. Then we were stateless refugees uncertain of what the future might hold for us; now we were returning to Europe as American citizens, full of confidence and hope.

A knock on the door interrupted our thoughts. Our steward, a handsome young Swede in an impeccable white uniform, had come to deliver a telegram. "How nice," I thought, "my parents in Baltimore are sending us a bon voyage greeting." I opened the yellow envelope and read "Jewish Social Service Agency has newborn. Reply immediately whether you want to accept. Love, Papa."

I handed the telegram to John and watched his face as he read the message. "What do you think?" he asked. Without hesitation I replied, "We can't turn back now. Let's wire them to assign the child to the next family on the waiting list." John hurried upstairs to send the telegram. When he returned, we hugged each other for a long time.

"This was rotten timing," he said, "but I am sure we made the right decision."

II

It didn't take us long to make friends among our fellow passengers, many of whom were Fulbright scholars en route to Finland. In preparation for their year of study they assembled every morning for two hours of Finnish lessons, and I was permitted to join them. At the end of a session I had enriched my vocabulary by half a dozen words. I would hurry to the library, where John could usually be found, eager to report my progress. Alas, by the time I reached him I had already forgotten half the words. There had been a time when I fancied myself a budding linguist, but that was before I encountered Finnish. As to Swedish, we were forced to learn enough to be able to communicate with our room steward, who spoke no English whatsoever. His favorite words were *aquavit* (a strong alcoholic drink) and *tack sa mycket* (thanks a lot).

Every effort was made to keep the passengers well-fed, occupied, and happy. Early morning calisthenics groups and shuffleboard and table tennis matches were organized to counteract the calorie-laden desserts, and there were nightly movies, travelogues, and an accordionist who accompanied those who wanted to dance. The lavish meals culminated in the captain's dinner, complete with large carved ice crowns with lit candles inside, and paper crowns for the passengers, to remind us of the three-crown symbol of the Swedish-American Line. On our last evening on the M.S. *Kungsholm* we were treated to a program of political humor by a well-known Swedish satirist. The audience showed its appreciation with wild applause and hearty laughter—all of them, except us. The entire program was in Swedish, and the jokes were untranslatable!

On Sunday morning, August 17, the M.S. *Kungsholm* docked in Bremerhaven in brilliant sunshine and a brisk breeze. Only a handful of passengers disembarked; the Swedes and the American Fulbright scholars continued their voyage to Sweden and Finland. We had formed close friendships during the nine days on the *Kungsholm*, and it was not easy to part. Our new friends stood on the deck, waving to us and throwing kisses.

Now the time had come for all of us to begin our separate adventures. We walked along the dock, following the arrows to the large building called Columbus Station. This is where the boats of the United States Line and the Swedish-American Line tied up. After the passport check and customs inspection, we exchanged some of our dollars for German marks. In those days the exchange rate was four marks to the dollar. It was easy to remember because the one-mark coin was about the same size as an American quarter. In terms of purchasing power, however, one mark was practically equal to one dollar.

Outside the Columbus Station a fleet of highly polished black Mercedes-Benz taxies was waiting for the Americans. "This is a far cry from our little Rambler," said John, quite overcome by the luxury of the taxi ride to our hotel.

During the war Bremerhaven had been heavily bombed, but modern, gray apartment buildings with brightly colored balconies had by now replaced the old, damaged houses, and playgrounds had sprung up out of the rubble. Nineteen years in America had almost made us forget how spotlessly clean the German streets were kept. Because it was Sunday, there was little traffic. The lack of noise and dirt made the scene appear unreal. Were we in fact back in Germany, or were we actors in a movie? On our walk we discovered what once had been a beautiful Gothic church. Now only the facade remained as a reminder of the evils of war. As John stepped back to take a picture of the ruins, a gentleman approached. "Isn't it awful what the British did to us?" he asked. "Perhaps you have forgotten what the Luftwaffe did to Coventry," John replied softly. The man turned abruptly and left the scene. Two wrongs don't make a right. Yet I was proud of John for speaking up.

We returned to our hotel in time for dinner. The meal of fresh fish was delicious, but we had no time to linger. Tomorrow morning we were to leave for Hannover where our search was to begin.

Our itinerary was to include Hannover, Frankfurt, and Hamburg, with a brief stop in Vienna and the International Congress of

Biochemistry. To give our nomadic life some structure we had established "anchors" in the three main cities. An anchor was a person who had agreed to let us use his address as a maildrop. We would check with him at regular intervals to report our next destination or forwarding address. Our first job was to notify our anchors of our arrival.

III

When World War II ended on May 8, 1945, with the German surrender, Germany and Austria were split into occupied zones by the victorious allies. The French occupied the area west of the Rhine; the British the northwest; the Americans the southwest; and the Russians the east. Each zone was headed by a military governor.

During the last weeks of the war the Allies had discovered the extermination camps that the Nazis had built all over Europe. Reports of the liberation of the survivors and the sight and stench of hundreds of thousands of unburied bodies in these places of inhuman torture received wide publicity in the Allied countries and caused an outcry for punishment of those responsible. In July 1945 the Allies formally agreed to prosecute the main war criminals for crimes against humanity. The most important trials were the Lüneburg Trials, conducted by the British in September through November 1945, and the Nuremberg Trials, conducted by the Americans from August 1945 to October 1946.

The American, British, and French zones made up West Germany, which was established in 1949 as the *Federal Republic of Germany*, with Konrad Adenauer, former mayor of Cologne, as its first elected chancellor. In July 1951 the U.S., Britain, and France announced the termination of war with Germany. After examining literally millions of cases, the Americans and British ended their de-Nazification efforts, and turned the purging of Nazis or collaborators over to the individual countries. In Germany the trials went on for decades, into the late eighties, while Austria made only minimal efforts to bring the criminals to justice.

In May 1955 West Germany became a sovereign nation, and the occupation forces were withdrawn. At that time the Federal Republic consisted of ten *Länder* (states) plus West Berlin, which were represented in the Bundestag (lower house) and the Bundesrat (upper chamber). Together the Bundestag and the Bundesrat constitute the Parliament.

In September 1951 Adenauer had won approval from the Bundestag to make amends for Nazi crimes in the form of material payments to Israel (reparations) and individual restitution to victims of Nazi persecution. In October 1951 the Conference on Jewish Material Claims against Germany, a group of twenty-two Jewish organizations, had been established to administer Holocaust survivors' compensation from the German government. In September 1952 Israel and Germany had signed the reparation agreement, and in 1954 Germany enacted the restitution law for individuals. The law lists four categories of restitution, for loss of (1) property, (2) freedom, (3) health, and (4) economic realization.

In 1956 the film *Night and Fog*, directed by Alain Resnais, was shown in Germany. It depicts the horrors of the concentration camps. In the same year the play *The Diary of Anne Frank* was performed in about a dozen cities in West Germany.

In 1949 the original Soviet Zone of Occupation had become East Germany, or the *German Democratic Republic*. At the time of our visit in 1958 it was far from being "democratic" or a "republic." In those days it was a communist dictatorship under the rule of the Soviet Union, totally separated from the *Federal Republic of Germany* by an impenetrable Iron Curtain.

It is important to keep this brief chronology in mind, for it was the historical and political events of the late forties and mid-fifties that formed the backdrop to our own unfolding drama. The social institutions of West Germany were straining to cope with the influx of more than ten million refugees from the east, those who had fled before the Iron Curtain came down and others who had escaped to the west in front of the advancing Soviet armies and decided not to return to their homes. Every welfare office that we visited displayed large posters with pictures of persons looking for missing family members.

In 1956 great efforts were made to enlighten the German public about its recent history. It was this consciousness-raising mission, undertaken by all the media, that was to enable many Germans to confront their past and their guilt. When we arrived on the scene in

1958 it seemed to us that most of the civil servants whom we met in our search were ready for us and that a few of them actually welcomed our presence.

IV

I will always associate the German railroads with my last train ride out of Germany. It was on the station platform in Berlin in November 1939 that I embraced my Aunt Paula and my grandmother, Flora, never to see them again. (After the war we learned that Aunt Paula had perished in Auschwitz in February 1943, and Grandma had died in Theresienstadt in the fall of 1942.) On that day the train, crowded with refugees and Gestapo agents, had taken us from Berlin via Hannover to the border, where we transferred to the Dutch train for Rotterdam.

And now, On Monday, August 18, 1958, we were standing on the platform in Bremerhaven awaiting the departure of the 10:18 A.M. express train to Hannover. By 1958 practically all the war damage to the German rail system had been repaired, and the railroads were restored to their legendary pre-war excellence. At first glance it seemed as if nothing had changed, from the official railway guide to the uniforms and hand-held signals of the train dispatchers. Actually there had been a number of improvements. Many of the old sooty steam locomotives had been replaced by sleek diesel engines. In our view, the most important change was the elimination of the third-class coaches. In the new democratic republic first and second class seats only were available to all.

Many European express trains have individual compartments that seat six or eight passengers in two groups facing each other. A sliding door separates the compartment from the narrow corridor, which runs along one side of the entire coach. We had no trouble finding a suitable compartment. It was empty but for a middle-aged gentleman. He immediately guessed that we were *Ausländer* (foreigners) and moved away from the window toward the center seat. "Would you like to have the window seats?" he asked politely. We gladly accepted his offer. Neither John nor I had ever travelled between

Bremerhaven and Hannover before, and so we enjoyed looking out the window, trying to read the names of the hamlets the train raced past. The first stop was Bremen, a city of over half a million people. Little did we dream then that we would visit Bremen again on October 27 under entirely different circumstances.

Dr. Gold, a restitution lawyer, was our Hannover anchor. Like many other Jewish jurists he had returned to his former hometown to help untangle the red tape created by the enactment, in 1954, of the Restitution Law. Thousands of Holocaust survivors, now scattered all over the world, were eligible for financial restitution, and the German bureaucracy responded with an avalanche of requirements and questionnaires. Only a skillful German-speaking lawyer was qualified to represent his clients in the negotiations and frequent lawsuits. Thus a new specialty was created, and one could find a Jewish restitution lawyer in nearly every major city.

Several members of John's family had entrusted Dr. Gold with the filing of their restitution claims, and there had been an ongoing correspondence between them. When Dr. Gold heard about our plans he agreed to serve as our "mail drop" in Hannover and also expressed an interest in our search.

When we arrived at his office Dr. Gold greeted us cordially and handed us letters from home that were waiting for us. It was good to know that our families were well and cheering us on. One look at Dr. Gold's office convinced us that he was, indeed, a very busy man. The cabinets were bulging with folders, and the files piled on his massive desk left only a small working area. The telephone seemed to be ringing constantly; a young man in an adjoining room apparently handled most of the calls. An elderly couple was sitting in the waiting room.

"This is my assistant, Mr. Klein," said Dr. Gold. "He will be happy to discuss your concerns with you," Dr. Gold added, as he ushered the elderly couple into his office. After all, adoption was not one of Dr. Gold's specialties, and Mr. Klein seemed to have more time to devote to us. Moreover, he was just about our age and, as we soon discovered, quite familiar with the needs of small children. He mentioned that he was married and the father of two lively pre-school boys. Apparently he already knew about our mission and volunteered to write a letter of reference for us. He explained that such letters of introduction were absolutely essential to open doors, not only to the youth offices of the welfare departments, but also to the individual orphanages.

He quickly typed a short letter on Dr. Gold's official stationery, signed it, and folded it neatly. Then he placed the letter into an envelope that he sealed carefully. Mr. Klein called the local *Jugendamt* (youth office) and arranged an appointment with the supervisor of adoptions. He handed John a file card with the address of the office and the name and phone number of the supervisor, and then he gave John the sealed letter. "Good luck," he said, "keep me informed of your progress."

John and I felt encouraged and energized. We decided to spend the rest of the afternoon wandering around town. Hannover, with about 530,000 inhabitants, had always been a lively industrial city with a long cultural tradition. Many of the original landmarks, dating back to the fourteenth and fifteenth centuries, had been damaged during the war. By 1958 most of them had been completely restored. Modernistic "skyscrapers" of about ten stories dotted the cityscape. Unlike Bremerhaven, which had impressed us with its quiet and immaculate streets, Hannover was bustling with people, bicycles, cars, streetcars, and neon signs. There were beautiful modern stores, ranging from small boutiques to large department stores, including Woolworth's. The streets were filled with pedestrians, and we joined the window-shoppers who were drawn to the tasteful displays of clothing, household items, and home furnishings. The outdoor cafes were crowded, and people seemed friendly and at ease. We had dinner at a vegetarian restaurant and returned to our hotel.

The next morning we met the supervisor of adoptions at the *Jugendamt*. We handed her the letter. She opened it, nodded approvingly, placed the letter into another envelope, sealed it, and returned it to us. "You will need this letter when you visit the *Kinderheim*," she said, as she beckoned us to sit down. "I have good news for you. There is a little boy at the home who is adoptable. His name is Anton." She studied our faces intently. "He has dark eyes, like you, and might just fit nicely into your family. We do not have many brunette children in this area, and I am glad that Anton is available."

"We would like to take a little present for the children. Do you think a large ball or perhaps a jump rope would be appropriate?" I asked.

"You don't need to buy anything. The children are well provided for." She looked thoughtful. "On second thought, it would be lovely if you could buy some bananas. The stand near the trolley stop sells them. They are fairly expensive. Three hands of bananas should be enough," she said.

She picked up the phone to inform the director of the home that we were on our way. "Don't forget the letter," she said, "and please come back to see me tomorrow to tell me of your decision."

Like most German orphanages, the *Kinderheim* was located on the outskirts of the city. An old-fashioned trolley snaked its way from the downtown area, past apartment buildings, to a development of individual villas, and through a wooded area until it reached a sunlit clearing. At the far end of a gently sloping lawn stood the orphanage. A gate in the picket fence marked the entrance to the property. "*Kinderheim zur Sonne*" (Children's Home in the Sun) proclaimed an enameled sign.

John was carrying a large bag with the bananas we had bought at the outdoor market. I checked my purse to make sure that the letter of introduction the social worker had typed for us would be readily available. As we approached the gate a large woman, clad in a white nurse's uniform, came to meet us. She opened the gate and extended her hand. "Welcome," she said as she shook our hands firmly, "how nice of you to bring the bananas. Please put them in the white basin over there," and she pointed to a small table. "The children don't get bananas very often," she said. "You must not be upset if they forget about their manners when they see these special treats."

I handed the nurse the letter of introduction. "We have come to meet Anton," I reminded her. "He is available, isn't he?"

"Oh yes," nodded the woman, "you will have a chance to observe him when the children line up for the treats."

Just then a side door of the main building was flung open and a group of about thirty children emerged. In single file they followed a young woman. She wore a gray dress topped with a dark blue pinafore. The children hopped and skipped behind her. Perhaps they had been told that some special visitors were to come. When the young woman with the pinafore had reached the table she said to the children, "These nice people over there have brought you some bananas. There will be one half of a banana for each of you. Wait in line. When I call your name, you may come to the table for your treat." She picked up a large kitchen knife, and as she estimated the length with her eyes, she carefully cut each fruit into two equal parts.

"Rosa, Emil, Frank, Ute, Anke, Marie, Hans, Klaus..." she called, and the children eagerly ran to the table to claim their shares.

We noticed that the children were all dressed alike in well-worn clothes. Each wore a gray apron with a large pocket across the entire front. The girls wore identical pink bands to keep their straight, blond hair from falling into their faces; the boys had the customary short haircuts; and all of them looked freshly scrubbed. One little boy, near the end of the line, looked different from the rest of the class. He had large brown eyes and unruly curls. "I think that must be Anton," I whispered to John.

"It's your turn, Anton," called the woman with the dark blue apron, "here's your piece!" Anton reached for the banana, smiled shyly, and hid it in his apron. He sat down in the shade of a large tree where he could savor his prize undisturbed.

The children wolfed down the banana pieces. Several had made their way to the enamel basin and began to examine the peels, hungrily searching for morsels that might have been left behind. The nurse in the white uniform, who had observed the feeding of the children, reprimanded them sternly. "There are no bananas left. The peels can't be eaten." The children listened silently. John and I looked at each other and felt guilty. We should have bought more bananas!

A little boy (was it Emil? or Klaus?) had made his way over to John and was clinging to his leg. "Hi there!" said John, lifting the skinny kid high into the air. "Do that again, please, uncle!" called the boy. John hesitated. In front of him a line of children had formed. "Me too, me too!" they shouted. John tried to lift each one. "Fritz," called the woman in the dark blue apron, "you are cheating. You already had your turn with our guest!" The child turned away in disappointment. Anton was among the few who had not come to be lifted up. He was still sitting under the tree, dreamily staring into space.

The woman in the white uniform had brought out lawn chairs and urged us to sit down. She went to Anton, took his hand, and led him to us. "Hi, Anton," I said cheerfully, "I bet you are three years old already," and I patted him on the mass of tangled curls. Anton sized me up, silently.

"He is a bit shy," said the director in the white uniform. "Actually he is four and a half now. He had a slow start, but he now manages to stay dry during the day. We hope he'll soon be dry at night, too." She seemed to sense that we were not impressed by Anton's achievement. "He does have a nice sense of humor," she added. "The teachers have told me that he likes to hide, and when he reappears he chuckles with joy. With his large brown eyes and brunette coloring he would fit nicely into your family."

She paused. John and I tried to engage Anton in conversation, but he remained silent and fixed his eyes on John's shoes. The woman cleared her throat, looked at us seriously, and said in a whisper, "Did they tell you at the youth office that Anton is a Gypsy?"

"That by itself is not what matters here," remarked John. We were turning to leave. "We will consider our decision carefully and discuss the matter with the social worker at the youth office," he said. "Thank you for letting us meet Anton," we said almost in unison.

The director of the *Kinderheim* escorted us through the gate and showed us where to catch the trolley to return to the city. We rode silently. "John, I am not sure I can handle this emotionally," I admitted at last. In my mind I saw the children, vitamin-starved and love-starved, begging for bananas and hugs. "I do hope that this experience will prove to be an exception, rather than the rule. What will happen to these youngsters?" I wondered. We decided not to adopt Anton. His eyes continued to haunt me in my dreams.

$$\underline{\underline{V}}$$

Although we had sent a telegram to our families in America on our arrival in Bremerhaven, we felt that after three days in Germany we had enough news to fill a whole letter. We tried to summarize our activities and impressions as best we could. John would provide a factual reporting of events, while I hoped to portray the personalities that played a role in our experiences. As our search gathered momentum, we noticed that while we lived the same adventure, our individual interpretations or reactions were often quite different in emphasis.

On Wednesday morning, August 20, we stopped briefly at the *Jugendamt* and informed the supervisor of our decision not to adopt Anton. We explained that we had serious doubts about Anton's ability (at the present stage of his development) to adjust to a new family, a new language, and the challenges of the fast-paced American way of life. We hoped that a suitable family situation could be created for him in Germany or another European country.

We had had an early start to keep the 8:30 appointment at the *Jugendamt* and had eaten the usual "Continental breakfast" offered by the hotel. It consisted of a roll with fruit jam and a cup of coffee, and provided little nourishment. I missed my bowl of crunchy cereal, milk, and orange juice, and the thought of a stack of pancakes with maple syrup almost brought on an acute attack of homesickness.

As we walked from the *Jugendamt* to the streetcar stop we spied a *Milchbar* (milk bar) where all kinds of dairy products were available. Its decor of fake marble counters and chrome-accented barstools seemed downright American. We decided to have an early lunch there. The food was inexpensive and the service was fast. If it hadn't been for the fact that the menu was in German and the waitresses said "*bitte*" (please) and "*danke*" (thank you), we could easily have imagined that we were back home or actors in an American film.

We studied the guide to the city of Hannover that John had bought at our hotel and realized that we were within walking distance of a park. It was a small oasis with benches arranged around a bed of colorful flowers. We had forgotten that in Germany it is strictly *verboten* (prohibited) to step on the grass, but were reminded by strategically placed signs. We sat down on a green garden bench to rest for a few minutes before beginning our brisk walk to the lawyer's office.

When we arrived, we found Mr. Klein on the phone and heard our name mentioned. "Sorry to keep you waiting," he said. "The supervisor at the *Jugendamt* was on the line. She told me that you had decided against filing adoption papers for Anton." He moved two chairs closer to his desk and asked us to sit down. "You must understand," he added, "that the *Jugendamt* represents only those children who are in public institutions or foster homes. There are, of course, also private welfare organizations run by the three religions. Being Jewish you may have difficulties, but it would certainly be worth trying to meet with a representative of the Caritas, the Catholic agency. The Innere Mission, representing the Evangelical Church (Protestant), may also be of help to you.

"Did you know that there is again a Jewish Community in Hannover?" he asked. I remembered reading that Jews had settled in Hannover as early as the thirteenth century. There had been ups and downs in the fortunes of the Jewish Community, but in the 1933 census Jews had made up 1.1 percent of the total population of the city. The lucky ones escaped before the Final Solution; the rest were deported and perished. I was amazed that in 1958 about 300 individuals who admitted to being Jewish had returned to Hannover. The great majority were elderly. Perhaps some had found the adjustment to the harsh life in Israel too difficult, while others had returned for economic reasons. Restitution money and pensions that had been earned before the Nazi era enabled many returnees to live quite comfortably. Mr. Klein called the office of the Jewish Community to inquire if a Jewish child might be available for adoption. We should have known that the answer would be negative. The few Jewish children who had been born after the war were treasures that would never be given up. After the establishment of the State of Israel, many

Jewish children emigrated to Israel, where they felt more at home than in postwar Germany.

Mr. Klein telephoned the Caritas in our behalf, but was told that our religion disqualified us. Yes, there were children available, but only Catholic couples were considered suitable adoptive parents. "Don't be discouraged," said Mr. Klein emphatically, "there are always circumstances when the regulations can be waived. You mustn't rule out anything."

Before we said goodbye, we gave Mr. Klein the name and address of our anchor in Frankfurt, and he agreed to forward our mail. Tomorrow (August 21) we would establish our headquarters there. We were planning to continue our search in the Frankfurt area until August 31, when we would leave for Vienna and the International Congress of Biochemistry. In our short stay in Hannover we had made a new friend and had learned lessons that would prove useful as we continued our search.

VI

The express train for Frankfurt was to depart Hannover at 12:45 P.M., and so we had the entire morning to ourselves. We used the found time to buy an overnighter at Woolworth's, returned to the hotel, and repacked our large suitcases. All the basic essentials needed for one or two days were transferred to the new smaller bag, which fit neatly into one of the large pieces. We were going to make Frankfurt our center of operations for ten days and planned to visit the youth offices of towns located within a hundred mile radius.

We stopped at the station restaurant for lunch and made our way to the platform, dragging our luggage. It was early and only a handful of travelers had gathered to await train D284 to Frankfurt, via Kassel and Marburg. Apparently Thursday afternoon was not a busy time at the station. An elderly lady and a girl with a backpack joined us in our compartment and immediately engaged us in conversation. Obviously we looked like *Ausländer* (foreigners) and needed to be educated, or so the older woman, a retired schoolteacher, seemed to think. When she discovered that we were headed for Frankfurt, her hometown, she launched into a lecture worthy of a tour guide. We learned that Frankfurt was the most important city in West Germany, that it was the greatest transportation hub, and that it had five railroad stations and the largest airport in Europe. In return we told her about the beautiful monuments in Washington and that we had come to Germany on business.

Soon the girl, a student at the University of Marburg, joined the discussion. She proudly told us about the famous *Messe* (fair) which had been one of Frankfurt's attractions since the thirteenth century. "You really *must* visit it," she urged. "There will be a fair in September, but if you miss that one, you surely *must* stay for the book fair in October," she added. She reached into her backpack and produced an aluminum container. "Here, have some plums," she said, offering the fruit to the teacher and us. "I washed and polished them. You need not worry," she assured us, "I used spring water. Did you know that when the Americans came here, they put chlorine in the water supply? My parents believe that the water was poisoned by the occupation forces. What do *you* think?" she asked John. He tried to explain that chlorinated water was actually safer to drink than untreated water, but he wasn't at all sure that he had convinced the ladies.

The train stopped in Kassel and very briefly in Marburg, where the student got off. The elderly teacher was quiet and we noticed that she had nodded off. John opened the folding table between the window seats and began reading the chapter on Frankfurt in *Fodor's Modern Guide: Germany 1958*. Promptly at 6:15 the train pulled into Frankfurt's main station. The platform was crowded with travelers, and apparently we were not the only *Ausländer* here. We were happy to see many American soldiers, and the sound of English was music to our ears.

Although the occupation forces had been withdrawn in 1955, there was still a noticeable American presence in Frankfurt. The U.S. Army Headquarters, the 97th General Hospital, and the main PX (Post Exchange) were located in the city, and American Express maintained several offices, including one at the railroad station. In the course of our search we were to spend many hours at the American consulate.

The international flavor of Frankfurt and its tradition of liberalism and culture endeared the city to us. After twelve years of Nazi rule, when all expressions of liberalism and tolerance had been stifled, Frankfurt had made a great effort to regain its spirit. The daily *Frankfurter Zeitung*, founded in 1856 by Leopold Sonnemann, a Jew, and silenced by Hitler, resumed publication after the war as the *Frankfurter Allgemeine* and today is again considered one of the great independent newspapers of the world. We stopped at the kiosk in the station and bought a copy of *The New York Times* and the *Frankfurter Allgemeine* before boarding a taxicab to our new home, Pension Feldberg, where our anchor, my Uncle Erwin Lichtenstein, had reserved a room for us.

VII

Pension Feldberg was a small inn located within walking distance of the Palmengarten, one of the most famous botanical gardens in the world. After 1955 the pension became the "home away from home" for Israeli families who had come to Frankfurt to pursue their restitution claims. Some Israelis would return to the unpretentious, homey inn year after year, for business reasons or to enjoy a respite from the desert heat. It was impossible not to meet fellow guests, whether in the shared bathrooms on each floor or at breakfast in the dining room downstairs, and soon everybody greeted everyone else in Hebrew, German, and even occasional English.

For us the main attraction of Pension Feldberg was Dr. Erwin Lichtenstein, my mother's younger brother, who had emigrated to (then) Palestine in 1939. Erwin had spent most of the years 1923 through 1939 in Danzig (Gdansk), where he worked as a journalist and lawyer. In 1933 he accepted the position as legal representative of the Jewish Community of Danzig, and devoted himself with heart and mind to saving the Jews of the city from the impending destruction. At that time the Community consisted of about 7,000 Jews. Under his guidance almost all of them were able to escape to Palestine and other countries, just days before the beginning of World War II, when Germany invaded Poland and the Free City of Danzig. Already in July 1939 Jewish ritual objects had been sent to New York. The contents of the ten crates would be exhibited in 1980 as "Danzig 1939: Treasures of a Destroyed Community," a testament to the vitality and culture of the Jews of Danzig. Beginning in 1956 Erwin Lichtenstein again became the legal representative of the survivors of the Jewish Community of Danzig. For twenty years he would come to Frankfurt during the summer months to defend his clients' restitution claims in German courts, and for many years he would make Pension Feldberg his summer residence.

When our taxicab pulled up to Feldbergstrasse 10, there was Erwin to welcome us. It was our first reunion since late August of 1939, when he, his wife, and three children had stopped briefly in Berlin on their way to Palestine. And what a reunion it was!

"Let's go out for dinner together," said Erwin as he showed us to our room. "I know a restaurant around the corner where we can talk." We were joined by Aunt Lotte and my cousin Ruth. In my eyes nobody had changed, and we seemed to pick up the conversation where we had left off nineteen years ago. Over soup and sandwiches we exchanged news and photos of our families, and then we all signed postcards to send home. It all seemed so natural and yet so totally unreal. "Don't order any dessert," said Erwin, "we have been invited to the Rosenberg's tonight. They are anxious to meet you, and they live close by."

Dr. Walter Rosenberg had been a physician in Berlin and had emigrated to Palestine in the thirties. He and Erwin had met at Pension Feldberg in 1956, when Dr. Rosenberg was considering setting up a medical practice in Frankfurt. They formed a lasting friendship. At the time of our visit the Rosenbergs were established in a lovely apartment, and the practice was doing well and growing. Moreover, they were adoptive parents themselves and eager to tell us of their own experiences and possibly to help us in our search. They promised to give us a list of persons to contact and to write that required letter of reference.

But now it was time for dessert. Mrs. Rosenberg had baked gooseberry tarts for us, a treat we hadn't tasted for over twenty years. It was late when we returned to our room at Pension Feldberg. We unpacked our overnighter (the large suitcases would have to wait), stopped in the community bathrooms located at opposite ends of the hall, and sank into bed. It had been a long day that had ended in a glow of warmth. At Pension Feldberg nobody had called us "Ausländer."

The next morning, Friday, August 22, we met my relatives briefly at breakfast and then started on our errands. We stopped at the office of American Express, where we had established a bank account prior to our trip and where a handful of letters were waiting for us. For lunch we met a social worker from the Central Office for Private Welfare Agencies. This lady had been a prewar colleague of a relative of John's, and she was delighted to hear how her old friend was getting along in the New World. Unfortunately she had few practical tips to offer. Her boss, who might have been able to advise us, was away on vacation. She suggested that we consult a representative of the International Social Service Agency, and she set up an appointment for us in the late afternoon.

And so we met Mrs. Braun over a glass of cider. She was pleasant and had come prepared with a booklet of instructions about international adoptions. We glanced at it briefly and realized that we would not be able to satisfy the many requirements in the short time we had available. Mrs. Braun wished us well, but warned us of the long and difficult road ahead. "Don't set your hopes too high," she said as we parted. We realized that we would have to blaze our own trail without help from private agencies or the International Adoption Service.

In the evening we had dinner with Erwin and his family. These meals would become almost daily events, and as time went on, they turned into therapy sessions for us. We would recount in detail our experiences of the day, and Erwin and Lotte would listen patiently to our report, offer advice, and sustain our spirits on days when our search seemed to turn into a frustrating wild-goose chase.

It was Friday night, and John and I remembered that in the "liberal" synagogues of Germany the main Sabbath service was held on Friday evening instead of on Saturday morning, as is the custom in many American congregations. We decided to attend services on the nearby U.S. Army post. When soldiers are far away from home, they tend to feel the need for spiritual renewal. Even those who rarely, if ever, attended Sabbath services at home would flock to the chapel on the base. John and I could understand this longing for identity, this reaffirmation of an ancient bond evoked by the familiar blessings and melodies.

Our rabbi had written to several Jewish chaplains in Germany to tell them of us and our search. It was a well-known but little talked-about fact that occasionally a young man who had gotten a girl into "trouble" would turn to a chaplain in the hope that the expected baby might be placed with a loving family willing to adopt it. At the social gathering after the services we introduced ourselves to Rabbi Greenberg, who had already been alerted by our rabbi. He agreed to see us in his office on Monday morning.

We suspended our search, and for one glorious, sun-filled weekend played full-time tourists. There was much to explore in the huge Palmengarten. Carefully tended walkways led from one special collection of flowers and plants to another. The colorful exhibits were neatly labeled and provided a feast for the photographers. A remarkable rock garden covered two and a half acres, and about a dozen greenhouses contained cacti of all kinds, insect-eating plants, and a complete tropical forest. The largest greenhouse, known as the Palmenhaus, was home to the Victoria Regia, the world's largest water lily from the Amazon. The temperature in the glass house must have been over ninety degrees Fahrenheit, and the humidity close to 100 percent. Visitors gasped when they stepped from the dry, brisk Frankfurt climate into the tropical atmosphere, but to John and me it felt just like home. The typical weather forecast for Washington, D.C. in August is "hot, hazy, and humid," and that's exactly what the Victoria Regia required.

We continued our walk a few blocks east to Grüneburg Park, which once had been the Rothschild estate. Now it was a public park with imaginative modernistic playgrounds and many benches. We watched the well-dressed, abnormally obedient children climb around a metal jungle gym in the shape of a huge elephant whose trunk served as a slide. All of a sudden, two lively youngsters shouting *"Eema, Eema"* ("mother" in Hebrew) ran toward a woman seated on a bench. She put her book aside and embraced the children. It was obvious that the youngsters, dressed in playclothes and sandals, were *Ausländer*. As it turned out, this Israeli family was staying on the second floor of Pension Feldberg.

Before meeting the Lichtensteins for dinner we stopped at the apartment of Dr. and Mrs. Rosenberg to pick up the information they had assembled for us. The manila envelope contained a list of towns near Frankfurt, names of officials at some of the youth offices, a few words of advice on how to field interviews with social workers, and, of course, the indispensable letter of reference. We had our work cut out for us!

VIII

For Sunday we had planned to take a sightseeing bus tour through Frankfurt, but we changed our mind. It would have interested us to see the Jewish ghetto, which dated back to the twelfth century and had once contained a flourishing community. But on the night of March 22, to the dawn of March 23, 1944, the *Altstadt* (old town) had been bombed by the Allies. Fires had raged through the old wooden buildings of the early medieval section of Frankfurt, and that included the Jewish quarter. A few majestic churches had escaped the bombs. By the irony of fate the bombing had completely missed the two great military targets of Frankfurt, the I.G. Farbenindustrie, notorious for its use of slave labor, and the industrial suburb of Höchst. Apparently an effort had been made to destroy them, but the bombs had fallen instead on the Rothschild mansion in the Grüneburg Park, demolishing it completely. After the war the United States High Commission for Germany took over the block of buildings that had housed the offices of I.G. Farben.

Between the years 1870 and 1933 the Jews of Germany were accepted as full citizens. In the liberal climate of Frankfurt they soon rose to positions of leadership in the areas of finance, journalism, education, science, and the study of Judaism. In the early 1930s Frankfurt even had a Jewish mayor, Ludwig Landmann. In March 1933, shortly after the Nazis came to power, he was forced to resign, as was the Jewish rector of Frankfurt University, the great center of learning that had been founded by Jewish philanthropists in 1914. The census of 1933 listed 26,158 Jews in Frankfurt. At the time of our visit in 1958 there were about 2,500, mostly concentration camp survivors and a few returnees from Israel and other countries.

The Frankfurt of 1958 was an architectural mixture of the very old and the very new, of ancient narrow streets and modern traffic jams. Some of the tourist attractions had been carefully reconstructed, incorporating original parts that had been salvaged from the rubble. The Goethe Haus, in which the great writer-poet was born in 1749, was an example of such work.

John and I decided to join a guided tour through this popular shrine. The presentations were given in English, French, or German and we opted for a German-speaking guide. He carefully pointed out the furnishings and paintings that had been part of Goethe's childhood, and then he paused. "Kindly arrange yourselves on this beautiful staircase," he asked the group of about twenty-five, "while I explain the mechanism of the grandfather clock that you see here." After a little shuffling the tourists found their places and focused intently on the clock. I didn't want to miss a word and cocked my head slightly. The guide looked up at me, pointed his finger in my direction, and said very slowly and distinctly, "Do you understand German? Can you follow what I am saying?"

"Oh yes, of course," I said, blushing as all faces turned toward me.

"Don't worry," John assured me, "it must be your American shoulder bag that makes him think you are an *Ausländer*. I'll buy you a new one in Vienna, and then nobody will pick on you again."

Unfortunately the solution to my problem was not so simple. During our stay in Germany I bought German shoes, a German sweater, and even a jaunty little hat, but I was easily identified as an *Ausländer*, no matter where I went. Not all such encounters were negative, however. One day, as we were leaving a bookstore in Frankfurt, a young woman approached me. "Excuse me," she said politely, "are you an Israeli?"

"No, not really," I laughed, "you are close, though. I am an American, and I happen to be Jewish!"

"I hope you don't mind my stopping you," the woman continued. "I just wanted to tell you that I feel terrible about what happened to the Jews. Is there anything I can do for you?" She looked at me searchingly. I gathered my thoughts.

"You might want to take a trip to Israel, or perhaps you might want to read a book on Jewish history. Then, when you hear anti-Semitic comments, you will no longer remain silent. I am afraid you can't undo the past singlehandedly, but you give me hope for the future." She held out her hand for me to shake; I took her hand into mine.

"Shalom!" she said softly and smiled. "Shalom! And thanks for stopping to talk with me."

Exactly one week had passed since we began our search, and although we had learned a great deal, we had made little progress. And so on Monday, August 25, we kept our appointment with Chaplain Greenberg on the Army post. "Let me tell you how I can sometimes help couples like you," he said as he opened a folder on his desk. "If I learn of a young woman who is pregnant by one of my boys, I can suggest to her that a couple might be willing to adopt her child. If she agrees to give up the baby, we use the services of a local lawyer who takes care of the legalities and makes the financial arrangements. Right now there is a girl who expects to give birth in late December. How long do you plan to stay here?" he asked.

"We have booked our return on the *Gripsholm* for October 29," replied John. "Perhaps we should meet with the lawyer and someone at the American consulate so that we'll have a better idea of what is really involved."

"That's right," the rabbi said, "I suggest you ask for Mr. Fisher at the consulate. He is a good friend of mine and very sympathetic to your cause." He wrote the name on a card. "Let me phone him and see if he is available today."

We were in luck. Mr. Fisher could fit us in at 11 A.M. We found him in the annex of the consulate and were immediately impressed by his ability to speak German and English with equal fluency.

"The most important step is to complete the legal adoption process," he said. "Once the child is yours, I can help you with the formalities of the immigration. You know, of course, that the child will need a valid German passport and a U.S. quota number for Germany and must be vaccinated before being admitted to the United States." He pointed out that Frankfurt itself was overrun with Americans looking for available children, and advised us to take our search to smaller towns and deal directly with the head of each local *Jugendamt*. "For a start try Bad Homburg, Darmstadt, and Giessen. There *are* children available, but locating them is a real challenge. I wish you luck," and he smiled.

We immediately liked Mr. Fisher and trusted his advice. In the next nine weeks he would become our most valuable friend and ally.

IX

Bad Homburg, a town of about 32,000, is located only twelve miles from Frankfurt and easily accessible by streetcar. Its eleven springs, which are said to possess healing qualities, were already known to the Romans, and from that time on the spa became a fashionable resort. At the beginning of the twentieth century Bad Homburg was known as a meeting place of Russian-Jewish intellectuals.

A small Jewish community existed there, and a synagogue was dedicated in 1867. Attached to the synagogue was a school building that is now being used as an adult education center. Inside the building, on a marble tablet, are these words: "Jewish citizens built this school behind the synagogue in 1877. Generations of young people were educated here. Crime and stupidity destroyed the synagogue on November 9, 1938, and damaged the school. On January 22, 1956, the Adult Education Center took over this building to work in it for understanding and tolerance." A photograph of the old synagogue hangs on the opposite wall. In 1933 there were 300 Jews in the town. Many of them managed to emigrate, and by 1939 only seventy-four remained, most of whom were deported to perish in the death camps.

We had made an afternoon appointment with Miss Schumacher of the *Jugendamt*. When we arrived promptly at 2:30 she was not in her office. We sat in the waiting room for what seemed an eternity and were just about to leave when a young secretary appeared. "There must have been a misunderstanding," she said apologetically. "Are you the couple who is interested in adopting a child? I have a leaflet here for you. It is written for Americans, and I am sure you will find it very helpful." She handed us four printed pages that listed all the requirements and regulations governing the adoption of a German child by an American family. The leaflet was dated June, 1956.

We thanked the secretary, and John carefully put the pages into his briefbag, next to the unused letter of introduction. There was no point in spoiling a beautiful sunny afternoon by studying the many rules, so we joined the crowds of visitors in exploring the Kurpark that surrounds the castle of the Landgraves, who had ruled the independent municipality of Hesse-Homburg from 1622 to 1866. After a while we made our way to the trolley stop for a leisurely ride home.

At Pension Feldberg the Lichtensteins were waiting for us. Erwin had discovered a Chinese restaurant within walking distance. We found a secluded corner table, and John and I began to recount our adventures. It had been a busy day, from the meeting with the chaplain to the visit to the American consulate, a quick lunch in a vegetarian restaurant, and the excursion to Bad Homburg. And after dinner, back at the pension, Erwin helped us interpret the four pages of instructions. Together we studied the leaflet point by point, marking the provisions that seemed most important.

In Germany it is required that a child who is to be adopted live as a foster child at the home of the prospective adopting parents for at least several months before the agreement of adoption may be executed. The local city or county *Jugendamt* (a part of the welfare department) must investigate the prospective foster parents before consenting to place a child in their home. As a rule, the entire process of foster placement and subsequent adoption will take about a year and a half. Applications from American couples who plan to stay in Germany for a short time only will not be considered by the authorities.

"We might as well stop reading right now," I muttered. "Look," John said, "it says here that the questionnaire for adoptions by aliens must be completed in quadruplicate! Oh yes, and copies of official documents concerning our marriage, health, finances, recommendations by superiors and church officials must be submitted to the youth office," John continued.

"A trial period of six months must elapse before the adoption agreement may be concluded. This agreement becomes effective only when it has been approved by the guardianship court and then confirmed by the county court having jurisdiction in the area," he concluded.

"We can't possibly satisfy all these requirements in nine weeks. It looks utterly hopeless," I sighed. Erwin shook his head silently. After a long pause he said, "I can't understand why the Germans would want to make these adoption procedures so difficult. There are hundreds of children sitting around in private and public orphanages all over the country, and one would think that most of them would be better off with parents, in private homes. On the other hand, I certainly see that the authorities want to be careful in sending children across the ocean with strangers. You do have all the required documents, don't you?" he continued. "I am sure you have experience filling out questionnaires in quadruplicate!"

"This is absurd!" Cousin Ruth interjected, "I had three children before I was twenty-five! Thank goodness, nobody made me fill out questionnaires!"

Erwin was still studying the instructions. At last he put down the pages and looked at us. "I don't think you should give up your search yet," he counseled. "After all, you have been here only a week. I believe that the personal interview is often more important than the formal papers. When the director of a *Jugendamt* sees how well prepared you are, how diligently you have translated all the American documents into German, how many letters of reference you are carrying with you, and how serious you are about this undertaking, he cannot fail to be impressed. You know how German officials value all the little details and how they love red tape. It makes them feel so important!" There was a broad smile on his face. "In my dealings with German courts I have learned that the individual judges wield great powers. A large area is left to the discretion of the court. Since there are so many prospective adoptive couples in the state of Hesse, the judges might be more inclined to stick to the letter of the law. Who knows, the judges in Westphalia or in Saxony might be more lenient."

I should have known that Erwin Lichtenstein was not only a skillful lawyer and the consummate diplomat, he also was the eternal optimist. He had managed to convince us to continue our search.

X

The day of our trip to Vienna was approaching, and so we decided to use the remaining time to the best advantage. We had made an appointment with the *Jugendamt* in Darmstadt, a town of about 125,000 located south of Frankfurt and easily reached by train. By now the routine was quite familiar to us: After a brief personal introduction we would explain the purpose of our visit, hand over one or more letters of reference, and hope for a referral to a *Kinderheim* where an adoptable child might be found. If the social worker handed us a printed form of instructions, we would know right away that the visit had been a waste of time.

The official at the *Stadt* (city) *Jugendamt* in Darmstadt politely heard us out. We had the impression that he was rather unsure of himself. Perhaps he had not encountered any Jews since the time of the deportations in the early forties, or perhaps he felt uncomfortable with *Ausländer*. He told us that he felt unqualified to deal with our request and suggested we visit Chief Inspector Korn, who supervised the adoptions for the county. "I'll make the appointment for you," the social worker said as he returned the reference letters to us.

Chief Inspector Korn's office was located in the same building. It was comfortably furnished and boasted a rug on the floor, befitting the rank of "Oberinspektor." Mr. Korn, a man of about fifty years, met us at the door and ushered us in. "Have a seat," he said as he walked to the impeccably clean desk and eased himself into his chair. "I understand that you are Americans and would like to adopt a child. I regret to tell you that, at the present time, there are no children available for adoption in this jurisdiction. Wouldn't it be easier for you to adopt a child in your own country?" We tried to explain that in America the demand for children was greater than the supply. "Oh, yes," he said, "you are not the first Americans I have seen in my office who have told me that."

There was a tone of authority in his voice and not the slightest indication of regret. He rose. "Maybe you should try the Caritas and the Innere Mission. Here are their phone numbers. I wish you luck." We thanked him for his time and headed for the door. Actually we had no inclination to linger in the office. All of a sudden some vivid and troubling images surfaced in my mind. The chief inspector had brought back memories of Gestapo personnel I had encountered as a child when my family had to apply at the police station for documents needed for our emigration. I was fully aware that the process of de-Nazification had been quite incomplete and that many members of the Nazi party had returned to their old civil service jobs after the Allied occupation forces were withdrawn.

"Don't let your imagination run away with you," remarked John, reading my thoughts. "I felt a bit awkward myself," he admitted. "When the man got up, I really expected him to click his heels," he chuckled. "Let's walk around the town. I need some fresh air!"

Darmstadt is a hilly town, and before it suffered heavy damage during the war, it must have been a charming place. In 1958 it was a mixture of ruins, medieval buildings, and a few very modern structures. The town itself had a long cultural history and was well known for its artists' colony, its writers and musicians, museums and libraries. Its Jewish Community, dating back to the sixteenth century, numbered 1,427 members in 1933. By 1938 about 600 had been able to emigrate. As was the case in many towns, there had been two synagogues in Darmstadt, one for the Orthodox families, and one for those of Liberal orientation. Both synagogues were destroyed in November 1938, together with all the Torah scrolls. We were not aware of any Jewish life in Darmstadt in 1958.

After a stroll through the town and lunch in the coffee shop of the new hotel, we felt ready to call the two private agencies Inspector Korn had mentioned.

We visited the Caritas (Catholic charities) first. The young lady who greeted us seemed genuinely interested in our search. But when she heard that we were Jewish, she had no choice but to tell us that the Caritas placed children only in Catholic homes. We had had the same experience in Hannover, and we should have known better than to contact the Caritas a second time. But our visit was not a total loss. The young secretary asked us about our life in America. Perhaps we were the first Jews she had ever met face to face, and we felt that our meeting had been cordial and educational. "Do go to the office of the Innere Mission," she advised us. "Their rules may be less restrictive than ours."

And so we continued on our rounds. The secretary at the Innere Mission (social service of the Evangelical-Lutheran church), Miss Hermann, seemed to be in her early twenties. She appeared happy to see us and listened to our story with empathy. "I do know of a little girl in a *Kinderheim* nearby," she said enthusiastically. "I think she'd be perfect for you. Let me call the home and see if she is still there," she said, reaching for the phone. "Great," she nodded to us, "I'll tell the couple!

"I think you are in luck, but let me check with my supervisor first before you make the trip to the home." She dialed and waited. The supervisor was called to the phone. "No," we heard Miss Hermann say, "they are Americans and they are Jewish." We watched the excitement fade from her face. "Yes, I do understand the rules," she said softly before ending the phone conversation.

She turned to us. "I am so terribly sorry to disappoint you," she said. "I really wanted to help you. I think you would have made great parents for little Lotte. I do wish they could bend the rules once in a while," she said with a pout. We assured her that we understood and, to switch the topic, asked her to recommend the best inexpensive restaurant in town. "Go to the Weinmichel," she said without hesitation. "All my friends go there. You will love their cider and their meatloaf with mashed potatoes." We thanked Miss Hermann and followed her suggestion. The food at the Weinmichel was indeed excellent!

We caught the 8:30 P.M. train to Frankfurt and returned to Pension Feldberg in time to tell Uncle Erwin about our day. "Another wild-goose chase," sighed John. "How long can we keep this up?"

XI

Our families had given us a "wish list" before we left on our trip. My father had requested boxes of the best cigars; John's father, an avid stamp collector, expected us to supply him with the latest issues of German and Austrian commemorative stamps; John's sister, a pathologist, had authorized us to buy a professional Leitz microscope on her account; and my mother had ordered a particular aluminum baking form that supposedly was unavailable in the Baltimore specialty stores. Each request required phone calls and time-consuming shopping trips. We decided to devote Wednesday, August 27, to purchasing the items on the "wish list" and some things for ourselves. John splurged on a new Mont Blanc fountain pen, and I acquired a stylish black French beret. Moreover, John had done the required translations to obtain a German driver's permit. As it turned out, he never used that valuable document during our entire stay in Germany. Public transportation by rail, streetcar, and bus plus a rare taxicab took us wherever we needed to go, even to the tiniest villages.

Before returning to Pension Feldberg we stopped briefly in one of Frankfurt's famous bookstores. To our delight we found the shelves stocked with works of Jewish authors whose books had been burned by the Nazis in 1933. It seemed that young Germans were eagerly discovering the "classic" writers and poets like Stefan Zweig, Emil Ludwig, Franz Kafka, Vicky Baum, Franz Werfel, Ernst Toller, and countless others whose books had been banned between 1933 and 1945. In those years the writer of "Die Lorelei," the romantic poem that had become a folksong, was referred to as "unknown" in the popular songbooks. We were thrilled to find "Die Lorelei" in a recent edition of German folksongs. The familiar text was unchanged, but its author was no longer "unknown," it was Heinrich Heine, the famous Jewish contemporary of Goethe and, possibly, the greatest lyricist of the German language.

In the afternoon we called the *Jugendamt* in Giessen to make an appointment with Mr. Schneider for the next morning.

Giessen, a town of about 60,000, is located about an hour's ride north of Frankfurt and considers itself the intellectual capital of the state of Hesse. It is known as the University City of Giessen, or, as the mayor's letterhead proclaims, the "City of Culture on the Lahn." Its Jewish Community can be traced back to the middle of the fourteenth century. In 1933 there were about 1,250 Jewish residents in Giessen; nearly 30 percent of them perished in the Holocaust; the rest escaped to havens all over the world. There had been two synagogues, one for the Liberal-oriented families, and one for the Orthodox. Both of them were burned down in November 1938.

During the second half of the nineteenth century and throughout the existence of the Weimar Republic, the Jews of Giessen played an active part in the intellectual and political life of the city. In 1933 about 10 percent of the faculty of the Ludwigs University were Jews, occupying positions in the departments of archeology, pharmacology, psychiatry, history, physics, geology, classical philology, philosophy, economics, political science, medicine, jurisprudence, mathematics, and sociology. As was the case at the University of Frankfurt, the rector at Giessen, Professor Richard Laqueur, was a Jew who was dismissed from service, as were all Jewish faculty members, when Hitler came to power.

Jews from Giessen held appointive and elective offices in every level of government, including the Reichstag of the Weimar Republic. It is quite remarkable that Jews were able to attain positions of leadership in all walks of life in a town that was known for its anti-Semitism, which predated the Nazi regime. In Germany many famous universities are located in small towns so that the students make up a sizable part of the total population. The student organizations combined an emphasis on fencing and beer drinking with a noisy nationalism, and traditionally excluded Jews from membership. In the twenties and thirties anti-Semitism on the campuses increased, and when Hitler came to power he was eagerly supported by most of the students as well as by an alarming number of faculty members. One can only surmise that this enthusiasm was echoed by the townspeople in general.

By the time John and I had reached adolescence, Jewish students were forbidden to enroll in German universities. Our visit to Giessen was to be our first exposure to a "*Kulturstadt*," and we looked forward to it with mixed emotions.

XII

We took the 9:11 train to Giessen and had no trouble finding the *Jugendamt*. Mr. Schneider was expecting us, and greeted us cordially. As we explained our mission, Mr. Schneider listened attentively but, unlike so many officials we had met, he made no effort to rush the interview. "I see you have brought along some documents and letters of reference," he said. "May I take a look at them? How thoughtful of you to bring the originals *and* the translations," he said smilingly. "I suppose you are familiar with the rules governing adoptions of German children by foreigners," he said as he took a copy of the *Instructional Leaflet* out of a folder. "It seems to me that your documents are very complete, and that should speed things up. However, I have found that item number four often presents a stumbling block."

(4) In cooperation with the International Social Service the Youth Office will make inquiries into the environments and circumstances of the prospective adoptive parents in their home country. References named by the applicants will be contacted for this purpose.

"In essence this means that the German *Jugendamt* requires a report of a home visit from a social worker in your American county or city *before* they will consider you as adoptive parents once an available child is found. But the *American* social welfare organizations usually will not make a home study unless the *German Jugendamt* is ready to approve the adoption and, at the same time, the German *Jugendamt* will not act on the couple's request unless the home study has been made. You can see that this creates a vicious circle. In German we have an expression for this kind of situation; we compare it to a cat trying to bite its own tail." He paused. "It is actually a very effective way to prolong the 'paper war,'" he said.

We explained that Mrs. O'Neill, the social worker in our county, had already met with us. She had been given copies of all our documents and the telephone number of a neighbor who had the key to our apartment. "I will get in touch with Mrs. O'Neill," he said reassuringly. "In the meantime I will give you a special letter that you should show to the officials at the youth offices. Be sure that the letter is always sealed and that it is returned to you sealed." He left the office for a few minutes. We heard him speak in a low voice to a secretary, and then he returned with a manila envelope marked "*Jugendamt, Universitätsstadt Giessen.*"

"We are so grateful to you," John and I said in one voice.

"I do not know of an adoptable child in my own jurisdiction right now," said Mr. Schneider, "but there is a little boy available in a *private* baby home in a village near Kassel. His name is Ulrich, I recall. Oh, yes, and you should also visit the *Jugendamt* in Kassel itself. I hear that there is a little girl available. She is supposed to be half-Jewish and very lively. Her name is Liesel Gelb." He rose and offered his hand. "I'll call and make the phone calls to save you time. Try to visit Ulrich this afternoon, and Liesel tomorrow morning. Good luck, and keep me informed," he said.

Armed with the "official" envelope that Mr. Schneider had given us and a resurgence of optimism, we set out in search of Ulrich. We took the train to Kassel, had a light lunch in the station restaurant, and then transferred to a local train. Unlike the express trains, whose coaches are divided into individual compartments, the cars of the local trains accommodate passengers in a series of parallel wooden seats. The backs of the seats are movable and can be flipped in either direction so that the traveler can always face toward the front of the train.

We found two adjacent seats and watched the coach fill up until almost every seat was taken. It seemed to us that the passengers, all men, were regular riders on this line. A number of them were carrying leather pouches with tools. Their faces, deeply lined, betrayed years of hard work. As the train stopped at every village or highway crossing, and as men got off at each station, we concluded that the workers were going home to their mid-day meals and, possibly, a short rest before returning to their jobs in one of the many factories in Kassel.

After about half an hour of stop-and-go riding, we reached a small town where we had to change trains. The new train, consisting of only two cars, was an example of modern "light rail." Brightly colored plastic seats, shiny aluminum handrails, and large clean windows gave it a utilitarian but cheerful look. The cars were filled with young people between the ages of fourteen and nineteen, loaded down with heavy bookbags. We were impressed by their quiet behavior and the serious expressions on their faces. We remembered from our youth that high school usually began about 8 A.M. and finished about 2 P.M. Students had their mid-day meals at home and once or twice a week returned to school in the afternoon for athletic games or extracurricular activities. We also recalled that studies were taken very seriously, for it was scholastic achievement that determined one's acceptance into the (free) university system to train for the professions or else into an apprenticeship program to prepare for a career in business or the skilled trades. Presumably the students on our train attended a central high school in the town after completing the basic grades in their local village schools.

By the time we reached our destination the train was practically empty. The station was deserted. We looked around for someone who might give us directions to the *Kinderheim*. John spotted a man in the faded uniform of a station attendant, and we doubled our steps to call attention to ourselves. The man noticed us and approached us slowly.

"Excuse me, sir," I said politely, "is there a restroom at the station?" The man looked me over. "Are you *Ausländer?*" he asked, eyeing me suspiciously. I couldn't figure out what that had to do with my question, but perhaps the man saw a relationship. "No, we don't have a restroom at this station," he said firmly, after giving the matter some thought. He turned to go. "Wait a minute!" John called, "we are visiting the *Kinderheim* and need directions. Can you help us?" The man obliged. "When you get to the bridge, you will see two arrows, one to the old part of the village and one to the newer part. Follow the arrow to the new village and continue for about one kilometer. You will see the *Kinderheim* on the right bank of the river. You can't miss it." He doffed his cap and disappeared.

We followed the man's instructions, and when we came to the bridge we found an idyllic scene. In brilliant sunshine the river stretched out in front of us. The clear water seemed quite shallow, and in the distance there was a small, rippling waterfall that had been created by a low dam. On the left the river had carved out a tiny pebbly beach where children were playing and fishing. On the right was a large box-shaped building, an ancient mill that had been converted into the private "infant home." We filled our lungs with the crisp, clean air. John stopped to take a photograph of the peaceful scene. "This is something to send home," he said.

It was about three o'clock when we arrived at the *Kinderheim* and were met by the director, a buxom woman in a white nurse's uniform. Mr. Schneider had already called her to announce our visit, and she seemed prepared for us. I was glad that she let us use the restroom without asking any questions, and then she led us into a very tidy living room and offered us tea and cookies.

"Yes," she said, "Ulrich is available for adoption. He is thirteen months old and taking a few steps. I will bring him out so you can get a good look at him. Please promise me that you will not touch him. We are very particular about the cleanliness and health of our children." She left us alone in the room as she went to fetch Ulrich. I noticed how quiet the *Kinderheim* was. "I guess this is the children's nap time," I said to John.

The director returned, placed Ulrich on the floor next to the massive table, and left. The child sat motionless and stared at us. We could not detect any reaction in his face: he did not seem afraid of us, nor was he happy to see us. He was dressed in a tightly fitting one-piece knitted suit that probably would have made any movement difficult. We talked to him and made cooing sounds in the hope that he might make an effort to crawl closer to us, but Ulrich remained glued to the place where the nurse had put him. Even the tiny plastic car that I took out of my bag and placed in front of him held no interest for him. He did not even reach for it. "Maybe the suit is too tight," commented John. We were starting to run out of ideas to communicate with him. I picked up the toy and put it back in my bag, and then we studied Ulrich's face. He was a cute little fellow, with very light blue eyes, straight blondish hair, and a very delicate, flawless complexion. "John, don't you think that his skin looks almost transparent? He looks as if he's never outdoors. I wonder if he has a vitamin deficiency?" I had read an article in a magazine about malnourished children, and Ulrich seemed to fit the picture. I was beginning to feel uncomfortable with our silent, motionless companion, when the director in white opened the door and removed Ulrich.

She soon returned and offered us another cup of tea. "How many children do you have in your care, and what is the age range?" John asked. We were told that the population fluctuated between forty and sixty and that the children were between six months and three and a half years. "I'll be glad to show you around the home," the nurse volunteered as she led us to the stairs. A young girl was scrubbing the old wooden steps with a stiff-bristled brush. She was on her hands and knees, and a bucket of soapy water stood by her side. The smell of disinfectant hung in the air. "Let's not interrupt Hilda. We take great pride in providing a hygienic environment for our charges. We can walk around the building and take the other stairs," she added.

There was still no sound to be heard in the home. "How do you manage to keep the children so quiet?" I asked.

"Oh, it's easy," said the nurse. "As soon as a child becomes noisy, we isolate him in a special room. He quickly quiets down. After we have done that a number of times, he no longer cries." She seemed very proud of this achievement.

We had reached the second floor and were shown a wooden deck that ran along the entire length of one side of the building. There were four square playpens on this balcony, each one containing four children who were hanging over the sides. They looked sweaty and listless.

"It's quite hot here," said John, "Do the children ever wear sun hats?"

"No, they get used to it," replied the nurse. I noticed that there were no toys in the playpens, and when I commented on that, I was told that toys would make the children fight over them. I got the picture: Toys lead to fighting; fighting causes noise; noise leads to isolation, and so on.

We descended the stairs and were glad to be out of the broiling sun. We returned to the living room. "When is the last train back to Kassel?" asked John. "I'm sorry we don't have the current time-table."

"Oh, dear," said the nurse, "you missed the last train. The next one leaves tomorrow morning at 7:30 to take the kids to school. We do have an inn in the village. Let me call up to see if they have a room for you."

We were relieved to hear that the Lion's Inn could put us up. We thanked the nurse-director for letting us see Ulrich and showing us around the *Kinderheim*. We used the restroom one more time and then headed for the main gate.

As we walked across the grounds we saw about a dozen children seated on one long, backless bench. We stopped near a group of trees, far enough away not to be noticed, and this is what we observed: Two young women, each carrying a large pot and one or possibly more spoons, walked slowly from child to child and thrust a spoon into their open mouths. The women walked back and forth until, presumably, the pots were empty.

"They might as well put these kids on a conveyor belt," mumbled John.

I could no longer contain myself and approached one of the wom-en. "These are the two-year-olds," she explained. "I feed them the farina and Inge follows with the applesauce," she added in a matter-of-fact voice. "It's quite efficient that way."

John and I left quickly. We felt we had seen enough of this depress-ing place. When I told him what I had just learned he turned very serious. "You see," he said, "it isn't just that these little kids are being dehumanized, but the staff actually are proud of their 'clean' and 'efficient' operation. I doubt whether even one of these kids can ever become an independent, confident human being. I really thought that the Nazi era was a thing of the past, but now I begin to wonder." We turned around and went back to the *Kinderheim*, asked for the direc-tor, and told her politely but firmly that Ulrich would not fit into our family.

XIII

When we left Giessen in the morning, we had no idea that we would need to spend the night in the village. Now the sun was setting and there was a chill in the air. We were glad that we had taken windjackets along, but we realized that we lacked the usual overnight items. "I've got to find a razor," said John emphatically. "Let's try to find a drugstore to buy the essentials." We walked back to the bridge and followed the arrow pointing to the "old" part of the village, the "center of town" that contained a general store, a repair shop for farm equipment, and the Lion's Inn. There was little business on a Thursday evening and, except for a horse-drawn beer wagon, the road was empty. We found everything we wanted at the general store: a chrome shaver with a swivel top, toothbrushes, toothpaste, a piece of soap in a plastic box, a small container of baby powder (deodorants were not available), face cloths, and a travel alarm clock. The man behind the counter packed the items in a large shopping bag with string handles and wished us a comfortable stay at the Lion's Inn. Apparently the word had already gotten around that there were two strangers in town. John asked if he might use the phone to notify our family in Frankfurt that we would not be returning home that night and not to worry. "We'll have a lot to tell you when we see you on Saturday," John promised.

The Lion's Inn looked like a medieval stopover for weary travelers. It had a large shingle with a painted lion's head on one side of the heavy door and a sign with a huge beer stein on the other. There was a bench out front where the locals would congregate to drink their beer and discuss the day's events. The innkeeper welcomed us, handed us a large iron key, and took us upstairs to our room. "This key will open your room and the bathroom door," he said as he pushed the five-inch key into the keyhole. John requested towels and toilet paper.

We washed our hands and faces in ice-cold water and went downstairs into the dining room. The innkeeper pointed to a chalkboard and rattled off the menu. We realized that we were hungry. Perhaps the hearty homecooked fare would cheer us up and let us forget the *Kinderheim*-factory across the river. I loved oxtail soup, especially if prepared with red wine, and the savory liquid, served in a heavy bowl with a piece of pumpernickel bread, hit the spot. The rest of the menu consisted of pork prepared in various ways and sauerkraut. We opted for a mushroom omelet with sliced tomatoes and a glass of malt-beer (non-alcoholic and very tasty).

"We need to get a good night's sleep," John said. "Remember, the train leaves at 7:30 and we have a little walk to the station. I'm glad we bought the alarm clock!"

We walked upstairs and turned the big key to open the door to our room. "You know, I have a funny feeling that this key opens every door in this inn, and maybe in other houses, too," I wondered out loud.

The beer drinkers downstairs had been joined by friends, and their loud voices and raucous laughter could be heard through the locked door. "I hope nobody comes upstairs to use the bathroom. I have always been afraid of drunks," I admitted.

There didn't seem to be a drop of warm water upstairs, and since we had already undressed, we couldn't even go downstairs to "borrow" a kettleful. We did what needed to be done and fell into our beds. "Ouch!" I cried. "The mattress must be made of wood! And the featherbed is going to crush me! This is camping medieval style!" I looked at John, who was already fast asleep. How I envied him!

I must have fallen asleep eventually myself, for I woke up in the middle of the night, shivering and bathed in perspiration. I had been having the most horrible nightmares: There were small children in bird cages. Someone handed me a huge iron key. I ran toward the cages to release the children, but the key was too big for the tiny keyhole. I wanted to cry out for help, but suddenly I was totally voiceless. John had disappeared. A man with a huge beer belly came running toward me. Thank goodness, I woke up. I forced myself to feel my way across the hall to the bathroom. Ah! The ice-cold water on my face felt delicious, and the soap had a delicate fragrance. I found my way back to our room, turned the key to lock the door, noticed that the luminous dial of the alarm clock showed 3:30, and crawled back under the lumpy featherbed. "Why are you running around in the middle of the night?" John demanded hoarsely.

"Don't worry," I said bravely, "I'll tell you tomorrow."

Both of us awoke before the alarm went off. We dressed quickly, packed the toiletries we had bought, and went downstairs. The pub and dining room were not yet open, and the innkeeper was probably still asleep. Since John had paid our bill the night before, we simply left the heavy key on the counter and stepped out into the brisk morning air.

We made our way to the bridge and stopped for another look at the river. The scene resembled an impressionist painting: the sun was just rising, and there was a light haze over the river. The little beach was deserted, and only a few ducks were out for a morning swim. We looked at the old mill that now housed the *Kinderheim* and sighed. It was difficult to reconcile the peace and beauty of the landscape with the oppression we had witnessed in the home.

When we arrived at the train station we joined a few students who had already assembled for their ride to school. The train pulled in exactly on time. It stopped every few minutes to pick up more students. Some of them looked at us as if they recognized us, but most of them were absorbed in a last-minute review of notes and books. When we reached our transfer point, the students gathered their gear and left quickly to begin another school day.

It was 8:40 when we arrived in Kassel. A beautiful new station had replaced the one that had been bombed out during the war. The restaurant was crowded with travelers who had stopped for breakfast. We were not in any hurry to catch a train, so we waited for a table for two and then relaxed over rolls and coffee. We needed to unwind before continuing our search in Kassel and Marburg.

XIV

Kassel, an industrial center of about 195,000 residents, is located in the northwest corner of the state of Hesse near its border with Westphalia. Its Jewish Community dates back to the thirteenth century, and in 1933 it numbered 2,301 members, or about 1.3 percent of the city's population. At the time of our visit, about seventy Jews were living in Kassel, and the beautiful synagogue which was destroyed in 1938 had not yet been replaced (a new synagogue would be built in 1965).

We followed Mr. Schneider's suggestion and made our way to the *Stadtjugendamt* in search of Liesel Gelb. The social worker was prepared for our visit. He told us immediately that Liesel had been adopted just one or two days earlier, and that there were no children available in Kassel at the time. We had the impression that the man considered our visit an intrusion into his work and time. As far as John was concerned, this experience was just another chapter in our wild-goose-chase drama!

We returned to the railroad station to find a train connection to Marburg, our next stop. Only eight days earlier we had passed through Marburg on the Hannover-Frankfurt express train, where we had shared a compartment with a university student. Our reason for stopping off in Marburg at this time was to make our acquaintance with this ancient and famous university town. Like Giessen, Marburg is located on the River Lahn. Its university was founded in 1527. Compared to the universities of Heidelberg (1386), Cologne (1388), Freiburg (1457), and Tübingen (1477), it was a relative latecomer. The universities of Giessen (1607) and Göttingen (1737) followed even later. All of these "centers of culture" shared certain characteristics and traditions, anti-Semitism being one of them. It was only a question of degree. With the exception of Cologne (1388) and Königsberg (1544), universities in the largest German cities were founded much later: Munich (1806), Berlin (1809), Frankfurt (1914) and Hamburg (1919).

Shortly after Hitler came to power, all Jewish staff members from all of Germany's twenty-three universities and from the entire public school system were dismissed. This was followed by the expulsion of all Jewish students. The question of relative degree of anti-Semitism was solved by making all schools *judenrein* ("cleansed of Jews").

My wish to visit Marburg, however, was quite personal. Erwin Lichtenstein's younger brother, Heinz Lichtenstein, M.D., had been a student at Marburg from 1924 to 1925. He had enrolled in classes with Professor Martin Heidegger, who taught philosophy ("atheistic existentialism") at the university from 1923 to 1928. One of his classmates happened to be Hannah Arendt, a young Jewess whom he knew from his hometown of Königsberg and who was to rise to fame in 1961 when she reported on the Eichmann trial in Jerusalem. Both Heinz Lichtenstein and Hannah Arendt transferred out of Marburg to other universities.

Marburg had been known for its strong philosophy department. Professor Hermann Cohen had founded the Neo-Kantian School in 1876 and taught there until he retired in 1912 at age seventy. He had then moved to Berlin to join Rabbi Leo Baeck at the School of the Science of Judaism, where he taught until his death in 1918. Cohen considered himself a "Jewish German" rather than a "German Jew," and apparently believed that Jews had a future in Germany as citizens of full equality.

Martin Heidegger, on the other hand, did not share Cohen's optimism. In fact, he had the dubious distinction of having been an ardent anti-Semite and Nazi since the 1920s, long before Hitler came to power.

There had been a Jewish settlement in Marburg since the early fourteenth century. In 1897 a synagogue was dedicated, and in 1933 the census showed a community of 325 members. According to information published by the City of Marburg in 1982 and 1992, the third and last deportation to the extermination camps left Marburg on September 6, 1942, at exactly 10:16 A.M.

When we visited the town in 1958, we were unaware of any Jewish presence.

Teaching faculties come and teaching faculties go, but the lovely scenery of this ancient town remained unchanged. We actually climbed the 140 steps to the *Schloss*, the thirteenth-century castle of the Landgraves, and then sat on a bench in the castle garden to wipe our brows and enjoy the breathtaking view of the valley below. We stopped in one of the little restaurants near the university and admired the ancient buildings and the modern, informally dressed students at the same time. The visit to the *Stadtjugendamt* proved futile, as we had expected.

We returned to the station via the 140 steps and were quite relieved to find a comfortable seat on the Hannover-Frankfurt Express. It had been a long and unusually warm day, and we yearned for a nice bath and comfortable beds. Only about eighteen hours had passed since we left Frankfurt, but it seemed that we had visited the Middle Ages. The train arrived in Frankfurt exactly on time, at 6:12 P.M., and we had dinner at the station restaurant. We took a taxi to Pension Feldberg, found our cozy room, and fell on our beds.

There was a knock on the door. It was Erwin. "I am sorry to bother you," he said. "You look as if you need a rest. But this package was sent here today by special delivery, and I thought it might be important. It's from a Mr. Schneider."

He handed us a flat, square box. John tore the wrapping off and discovered a two-pound box of delicate chocolates. "Wow," he exclaimed, "these are my favorites. I haven't seen this brand since 1939," he gasped. "Why in the world would Mr. Schneider do such a thing?" we wondered.

"Maybe he liked you," offered Erwin. "Let's talk about it tomorrow," he said chuckling as he closed the door behind him.

XV

Saturday, August 30, marked the end of our second week in Germany. We had seen and learned a lot during that time, but as far as our search was concerned, we had made hardly any progress. The warm bath and good night's sleep had restored us physically, but the mental image of the abnormally quiet *Kinderheim* and the unresponsive face of little Ulrich could not be erased so readily.

When we met the Lichtenstein's for midday dinner, we were able to keep them spellbound with our dramatic story. As Erwin later commented, it had all the elements of a gripping play: striking scenery, memorable characters, suspense, and even a surprise ending. As we tried to sort out our impressions and reactions we were grateful to our audience, who indicated their support by alternately nodding in agreement or shaking their heads in disbelief.

As the waiter brought out the apple strudel with whipped cream, cousin Ruth asked, "What are your plans for tomorrow?" With all the talk about the past, we had neglected to mention the immediate future! On Sunday morning we were to leave for Vienna and the Fourth International Congress of Biochemistry. It was time to return to the reality of train schedules and overstuffed suitcases.

Aunt Lotte gave me a big hug. "I hope you have a great time in Vienna," she said. "Enjoy yourselves and tell us all about your trip when you come back next Sunday. Be well!"

"Try to get tickets for the theater or opera. Make the most of your stay in Vienna," advised Uncle Erwin.

"Go easy on the desserts," laughed Ruth. And while the Lichtensteins returned to the pension for their afternoon nap, we took a streetcar to the American Express office to exchange some of our dollars for Austrian schillings. We also picked up several travel brochures and maps of southern Germany and Austria, including a map of the city of Vienna.

Neither John nor I had ever visited Vienna, and we were looking forward to this great experience. To prepare for our visit, we had read about the history of Vienna and specifically about its Jewish Community. We learned that Jews had been present in Austria as early as the tenth century and that Vienna's first synagogue was opened in 1204. The history of the Jews in Vienna and other towns in Austria consists of a series of ups and downs, invitations to Jews from neighboring countries to settle in Austria alternating with periodic pogroms and expulsions. The Vienna synagogue was destroyed about 1420, and its stones were used in the building of the University of Vienna. By the late eighteenth century there were about 1,000 Jews in Vienna, and in 1811 a public synagogue was authorized. Between 1875 and 1914 Jewish authors and composers helped make Vienna a literary and musical center.

Unfortunately Vienna also had the distinction of being the birthplace of anti-Semitism as a political force, long before the birth of Hitler. In 1895, Karl Lueger, a rabid anti-Semite, was elected mayor of Vienna, and the liberal movement, which counted many Jews among its leaders, suffered a significant setback. While some Jews reacted to the events by converting to Christianity, others joined the political Zionist movement founded by Theodor Herzl.

Yet the Jewish Community of Vienna continued to grow, thanks to a steady stream of immigrants from Moravia, Bohemia, Poland, Hungary, and Romania. In 1933 there were about 200,000 Jews in Vienna, approximately 10.5 percent of the entire population, and Vienna enjoyed a worldwide reputation as a cosmopolitan cultural center. All this changed with the ever-growing surge of Nazism, culminating in the *Anschluss* (annexation) of Austria by Germany in March 1938 and the ensuing anti-Jewish terror. Many Jews committed suicide, thousands fled, and of the 70,000 who were still in Vienna in 1939, practically all perished during the Holocaust in concentration and extermination camps. By 1942 Vienna was "*judenrein.*"

After the war a tide of 200,000 Jewish refugees passed through Vienna on their way to Israel, and in 1956 thousands of Jews fled Hungary after Russian troops had crushed an anti-communist revolt. When we visited Vienna in 1958, an organized Jewish Community of about 10,000 was again in existence.

On Sunday, August 31, we boarded the *Donau Kurier*, the train that was to take us from Frankfurt to Vienna. It was 11:23 A.M. when we settled in our compartment for the ten-and-a-half-hour train ride. We were carrying sandwiches and fruit and a bag of Mr. Schneider's exquisite chocolates. Sodas and complete dinners were to be bought on the train. We leaned back and relaxed as we passed through the countryside, stopping in Würzburg, Nürnberg, and Regensburg. All these cities were new to me, but to John, who had been stationed with the American occupation forces near Nürnberg in 1946, the landscape brought back memories. About twenty-five kilometers before the train reached the border town of Passau, the tracks began to run alongside the Danube (Donau) River, offering the passengers breathtaking views. We arrived in Passau at sunset and managed to capture the picture with our primitive 8-millimeter movie camera.

The train remained in Passau for a few minutes to give the Austrian crew sufficient time to replace the German officials. There was the usual passport inspection, but this time it held no terror for me. I was the proud owner of a U.S. passport, not the stateless refugee who had crossed the German border into Holland in November 1939.

Once the train had pulled out of the station, we set out in search of the dining car. We had read about the fabulous food and romantic atmosphere of the inter-European diners and were eagerly anticipating a meal of schnitzel and Linzer torte. But where was the diner? We walked back and forth, refusing to acknowledge that there was no diner on this train. The German dining car had been unhooked at Passau, but it had not been replaced by its Austrian counterpart. It dawned on us that the modest lunch we had consumed near Würzburg would be our last meal for a long time.

We arrived in Vienna about 10 P.M. and discovered that the station restaurant was closed and the kiosks where hot dogs and beef broth were sold during the day were tightly shuttered. We would gladly have settled for a candy bar, but even that was unobtainable. My spirits were sagging when a stylishly dressed lady approached me. "Excuse me," she said, "I am a stranger here. Could you please tell me the best way to get to Beethovenstrasse?" she asked in perfect German. I hesitated for only a minute. "I am so sorry," I said, "I am a stranger here myself."

I doubled my steps to catch up with John, who was dragging the large suitcase toward the exit. "John," I said breathlessly, "would you believe that in Vienna I am not labeled *Ausländer?* It seems that everyone is an *Ausländer* here!"

"Well, maybe not everyone," John commented, "but certainly the majority of the five thousand scientists who will be attending the International Congress tomorrow. Now, where will we find a taxi to take us to our lodgings?"

We left the station and joined a large group of weary travelers who had assembled under the sign *"Taxen."* No taxi was in sight.

XVI

In order to save money, we had opted to stay with a private family in Vienna, rather than in a hotel. When a number of taxi cabs drove up at last, the drivers called out the names of the hotels and the riders lined up to form groups. The cabs filled up and drove off, leaving John and me alone on the deserted sidewalk. Time passed. At last, about 11:15, a driver appeared, took pity on the two of us, and loaded our luggage in the trunk. We explained that our destination was an apartment house on Streichergasse in Vienna's Third district.

"I've never heard of such a place," the man mumbled, shaking his head. "Are you sure there is such a street in the Third District?" he asked, as he turned around leaning over the back of the front seat. "All right, I'll take you to the Third District, and maybe we can study the street signs."

"This doesn't sound very promising," I whispered to John. We were quite sure that the address, which had been supplied by the Tourist Office, was correct.

The name Streicher was well known to us as belonging to one of Hitler's infamous henchmen. At the Nuremberg Trials in 1945 Julius Streicher, the leading Jew-baiter, had been condemned to death by hanging. It was reported that he had been defiant to the end, and when he mounted the steps of the gallows, he called out *"Heil Hitler!"* And now, by the irony of fate, we were looking for a street bearing this murderer's name, in the middle of the night, in Vienna's Third District!

We drove around in circles until the driver stopped under a street lamp. "Do you have a map?" The man sounded desperate.

"Oh, yes," replied John, unfolding the tourist map we had bought in Frankfurt. John was able to locate Streichergasse and began to direct the hapless driver. *"Rechts!"* (right) he shouted. "Now *links*" (left), as we proceeded at a snail's pace.

It was midnight when we pulled up at Number 9. The driver deposited our luggage on the sidewalk and broke the eery silence by banging on the locked front door. I had visions of having to spend the night outdoors, when I heard footsteps. Mrs. N., our landlady for the week, had been waiting up for us. John paid the driver generously, and we followed Mrs. N. up a flight of stairs to the apartment.

We rose early the next morning and joined two Australian biochemists at breakfast. They knew no German and made efforts to communicate with Mrs. N. in French. John and I assumed the role of interpreters.

Mrs. N. was delighted that she could confide in me in her own language. For years she had suffered under the Russian occupation, an innocent victim of uncivilized troops, she complained in a whiny voice. We had been warned that there were two types of Viennese, those who complained about the Nazi takeover, and those who complained about the Russian occupation. A simplistic interpretation categorized the former as communists and the latter as Nazis. I therefore concluded, rightly or wrongly, that Mrs. N. was a Nazi, and I tried to avoid her as much as possible.

The meetings of the International Congress were held at the University of Vienna, where people of all races and nationalities had assembled peacefully in the pursuit of science. There were representatives from all parts of the world, including those behind the Iron Curtain. The atmosphere, intellectually and socially, was exhilarating. John enjoyed the lectures and fellowship with old friends and colleagues, while I went sightseeing with the wives of some of the scientists. For both of us there was even time for hiking, apple cider tasting, visits to coffeehouses, a concert, and lots of people-watching. A Gypsy band in a Hungarian restaurant reminded us of little Anton, whom we had met in the orphanage near Hannover.

Although we had little hope of finding an adoptable child in Vienna, we visited the social service offices of the Jewish Community (*Kultusgemeinde*) and the Joint Distribution Committee. We were told that an adoption would require two and a half to three years, *if* children were available. But there were none.

On Sunday, September 7, we left Vienna on the *Donau Kurier* for Frankfurt to resume our search. Three weeks had passed since our arrival in Germany, and we had not made any progress. Realizing that time would soon be running out, we set a deadline for our search: If we had not found an adoptable child by September 21 (the end of the fifth week), we would abandon our quest and devote ourselves completely to tourism.

XVII

On our return to Frankfurt we threw ourselves with renewed energy into our pursuit. We returned to Rabbi Greenberg, the chaplain on the Army base, to find out if there had been any new developments. There were none. Rabbi Greenberg urged us to make an appointment with the prominent lawyer in Frankfurt who handled all adoptions for Americans. Apparently this lawyer was in touch with the chaplains on *all* military bases in Germany and had been very successful in finding babies and arranging for their adoption. We phoned to make an appointment with the lawyer and were told that he was too busy to see new clients. His secretary would be happy to talk to us, however, at least for the initial interview.

We went to the lawyer's office the next day. The waiting room was filled with English-speaking clients. "Business seems to be great," muttered John. "I wonder what the fees are."

The secretary ushered us into her office and began to explain the adoption procedure. "We are quite familiar with the laws concerning the adoption of German children by foreigners," said John. "Could you explain the costs involved?" The secretary handed him a printed brochure, and as he read the information his face tensed up and turned red.

"I don't think we can afford such an expense," he said firmly as he returned the brochure to the secretary.

As we were leaving her office, a woman in the waiting room rose from her seat and approached us. "I am Selma Cohen from New Jersey," she said. "Like you, I am searching for a child, and I'd love to talk with you about your experiences. Perhaps we could have dinner together?" She handed us a slip of paper with her address and phone number, and we agreed to meet her that evening.

Over a plate of chicken fricassee Mrs. Cohen revealed her story. Four years ago the lawyer had helped her with the adoption of a little girl. It was a beautiful child, a dream come true. Mrs. Cohen's eyes filled with tears. "She died three months ago of leukemia," she said, weeping quietly. "I have returned to Frankfurt to find another little girl to replace Edith," she said. "I know the lawyer will find another baby for me. I am willing to stay in Germany as long as I need to. Money is no obstacle." She wiped her eyes.

John and I realized that Mrs. Cohen was determined to fill the void left by Edith's death, and since she spoke no German, she was totally dependent on the lawyer's services. She envied our ability to conduct our own search and deal directly with German social workers. We had the feeling that she considered us rivals. Why had she been so eager to meet with us?

"It must be very difficult for you to have to go through this again," I said.

"You have no idea how lonely I am," she replied. "I hate being here by myself for who knows how long, even though I call my husband every night. And yet I cannot face going home without a little girl. You understand, don't you?" she asked anxiously.

"Perhaps it is too soon after Edith's death to search for another child," I said gently. "You ought to regain your equilibrium first. Babies are so demanding," I added.

She nodded. "Could we meet again soon?" she pleaded.

John assured her that we would not be competing with her. "We do not have the money to deal with the lawyer. There is really no difference between the 'gray market' in America and this lawyer's method," he said. "We will continue our search on our own. If we come across a *Jugendamt* that has a surplus of adoptable children, we will certainly get in touch with you," he added. We parted without setting another dinner date.

The next day we visited another *Kinderheim* in a small town northwest of Frankfurt. The social worker at the *Jugendamt* had indicated that the children in this home were "older," ranging in age from three to six years. She seemed delighted when we told her that we were willing to consider an older child. We figured that it might be easier to assess the child's physical, mental, and emotional development than it would be with an infant. The social worker gave us directions to the home and phoned the director to announce our visit.

It was drizzling as we walked to the home, a building right in town. It looked like a school, and in the back there were swings and sandboxes, but because of the rain, all the children were inside when we arrived.

We were welcomed by a vivacious woman who was not wearing a nurse's uniform. She led us into a spacious room. About twenty children were seated on the floor in a large circle. "Would you like to join us?" she asked. "We were playing Drop the Handkerchief. Gudrun, explain to our visitors how we play the game," the teacher said, pointing to a chubby red-haired girl of about four. The child stood up, moved to the center of the circle, and told us in which direction to run in case someone dropped a handkerchief behind us. "That was a good job," the teacher said approvingly. Gudrun beamed. John and I took our places on tiny chairs that the children had provided for us, and before long John was running around the circle. He dropped the handkerchief behind a giggly dark-haired boy. The child had been looking at me with great interest. Something about me seemed to fascinate him. Perhaps he sensed that I was just about to fall in love with him. He picked up the hanky that John had dropped behind him, ran around the circle, and dropped it behind me. I wasn't even surprised.

I kept looking at John, who seemed quite at ease with the children. The atmosphere in the room was like that in any American nursery school. The only difference was that the children spoke German and seemed better behaved than their American counterparts. When all the children had had a turn, the teacher suggested another circle game. This one seemed very much like The Farmer in the Dell, although the words were different, of course.

John signaled to me that he wanted to leave. I followed him to the director's office. "What do you think?" he asked. "This is some change from the other orphanages we have seen!" he said.

"Yes, these kids seem happy," I said. "John, I have fallen in love with that little boy, you know, the one who dropped the hanky behind me. Did you notice that impish smile?"

"Sure," said John. "I think his name is Peter. Let's ask about him."

A young aide took over the supervision while the vivacious teacher ushered us into her office. "Could you tell us a bit about Peter?" John asked.

"Well, Peter is four and a half and a rather bright little fellow. Unfortunately he is not available for adoption. He is with us only temporarily. His mother, a single woman, had to undergo major surgery. She left Peter with us, and he has adjusted quite nicely. When she is strong enough to manage, he will leave us. We hope his mother will have a good recovery and he can go home soon. But we'll miss Peter," she said."

"Actually we don't have any adoptable children right now," she continued. "Perhaps you can check with us again in about a month. There may be changes in the legal status of one or two of our children by then.

"It will be too late for us," I said sadly. "We have booked passage on the liner for October 29. We must return to America, and it may have to be without a child."

"Thank you for having us. We enjoyed our visit," said John as we left.

The rain had picked up, and we walked briskly to the train station. As we reached the platform the train to Frankfurt was pulling in. We found two seats. "John," I said, "do me a favor and don't call this visit a wild-goose chase. It was not a waste of time. I just realized that there can be an orphanage with happy children. I hope we can find another one like this one soon, even if we can't find another Peter."

XVIII

On Friday, September 12, we continued our search in Friedberg and Hanau. At each *Jugendamt* we were handed the same lengthy questionnaire for the International Social Service Agency that we had encountered earlier, and were assured that there was not a single child available in the three children's homes in the area. By now we had seen about one hundred children who were waiting in orphanages. Waiting for whom? Waiting for what? Waiting for how long? We surmised that unless German adoption requirements were radically changed, a dismal future lay in store for these children.

With each passing day John and I found it more difficult to maintain our optimism in the face of constant disappointment. While we were grateful for the support of our relatives and enjoyed the interesting excursions to the Frankfurter Messe, museums, and the excellent library in the Amerikahaus, we realized that there was no hope of finding a child in the Frankfurt area. We were considering the possibility of going back to North Germany and trying our luck in the former British zone of occupation.

And then a miracle happened! On Saturday, September 13, we received a letter that was to change the course of our search. It came from Lüneburg, a town southeast of Hamburg. It advised us that two girls were presently available for adoption.

We were dumfounded! How did the *Jugendamt* know of us? Who had informed it of our address and our search? Was it possible that our "connections" in Hannover had notified the *Jugendamt* in Lüneburg? Or did Mr. Schneider, the social worker in Giessen, have anything to do with our good fortune? Neither Dr. Gold in Hannover nor Mr. Schneider in Giessen admitted to any involvement in this development, and the letter itself provided no clues to our questions. To this day we have no idea who or what prompted this letter to be sent to us at a time when our spirits had sunk to their lowest level. I have experienced many strange coincidences in my past, and I have learned to accept these unsolved mysteries as special blessings in my life.

John and I took time out to sit in the sun in Rothschild Park and make plans for the future. Suddenly the world seemed brighter. John cautioned me not to become too enthusiastic. "We've been on many wild-goose chases before," he warned me, "and you tend to go on emotional roller coasters. Try to conserve your energy. It will take a couple of days to wind things up here in Frankfurt."

The next day was the eve of Rosh Hashanah, the beginning of another Jewish year. Rosh Hashanah and Yom Kippur (Day of Atonement) are the most solemn Holy Days in the Jewish calendar. Even those who, during the year, profess no ties to their tradition flock to the synagogue to spend these days in prayer and introspection. Synagogues and temples all over the world are filled to overflowing with these three-day Jews who feel the need to hear the piercing sounds of the *shofar* (ram's horn) and to renew their ties to the "Remnant of Israel." I had attended High Holy Days services since I was eleven years old; and 1958 wasn't going to be any different, especially since I was feeling a bit homesick for my family and my congregation in America.

We decided to attend the Rosh Hashanah service at the U.S. Army base, where our chaplain-friend, Rabbi Greenberg, was officiating. The hall was filled with young men in uniform. Some of the soldiers had come in from as far away as Bremerhaven and Berlin. I looked around the room, studying the serious young faces, when I recognized Selma Cohen from New Jersey. She looked drawn and tired. I was sure her feelings of loneliness were intensified during the holiday season, and it was comforting for her, as it was for me, to attend an American-Jewish service far away from home.

Rabbi Greenberg's sermon was short and to the point; a cantor blew the *shofar* and led the congregation in the familiar melodies; and when the service was over the worshippers gathered in small groups to share some refreshments. We spotted Mrs. Cohen in a long line of people waiting to shake hands with the rabbi. She had noticed us and waved. We made our way through the crowd. "Selma," I said, "we are leaving on Tuesday to continue our search in northern Germany. We wish you all the best!"

She gave me a big hug. "Be well," she said. "I'll miss you!" she added, shaking John's hand as we inched our way toward Rabbi Greenberg. We informed the rabbi of the new developments in our search and thanked him for his efforts on our behalf. "You are off to a good start in the new year," said the chaplain and smiled.

The following day we were unable to attend the morning services. There was simply too much to do in preparation for our move on Tuesday. Since Lüneburg falls under the jurisdiction of the U.S. consulate in Hamburg, John notified the American authorities there of our search. He also made reservations at the best hotel in Lüneburg.

We decided to visit Mr. Schneider, the social worker in Giessen, to see if the documents from our local welfare department in America had arrived. The report of a home visit and its approval by the county office were absolutely essential for the legal adoption of a child in Germany. Mr. Schneider was disappointed that there had been no reply from Mrs. O'Neill, and he urged us to send a cable reminding her of the importance of his request. "With the legal obstacles you will have to overcome once you find a child, it is unthinkable that the lack of a home study report should keep you from reaching your goal. It really upsets me to think that just because one individual drags her feet, the whole undertaking could come to naught. I will of course, send another letter to Mrs. O'Neill, but a telegram from you will be faster and more effective," Mr. Schneider said. We realized that his support went beyond the call of duty. Apparently he was taking a very personal interest in us. "Do keep in touch with me," he said. "I'll try to help you in any way I possibly can. Good luck to you!" he said as we shook hands and prepared to leave.

We returned to Frankfurt for a festive dinner with the Lichtensteins, paid our bill to Pension Feldberg, made arrangements to have our mail forwarded to our "anchor" in Hannover, and devoted the rest of the evening to packing.

On Tuesday, September 16, we moved to Lüneburg, the beautiful medieval town on the Ilmenau river, that was to be our home for the next five weeks.

XIX

Before continuing our story, I must digress briefly to describe a period of history which, in my opinion, directly affected the outcome of our search. It concerns the role that the city of Lüneburg played in relation to the Nazi concentration camp at Bergen-Belsen and the subsequent British war crimes trials known as the Lüneburg Trials. My summary is based on German reports and documents I found in the library of the U.S. Holocaust Memorial Museum in Washington, D.C., which are listed in the bibliography at the end of this book.

"Transit Camp Bergen-Belsen," a Nazi concentration camp that has been likened to Dante's Inferno, is located in northern Germany between Hannover to the south and Hamburg to the north. The map shows approximate distances of fourteen miles to Celle, thirty-four miles to Hannover, and forty miles to Lüneburg. About 100,000 innocent people perished there of starvation, disease, and torture, including about 37,000 Jews and about 50,000 Soviet prisoners of war.

Bergen-Belsen was built in 1936 to house workers who were to construct quarters for German troops who used the area for maneuvers. In 1940 it became a prisoner of war camp for about 600 French and Belgian prisoners. By the fall of 1941 the camp had been expanded to house about 14,000 Russian prisoners. Epidemics of dysentery and typhus decimated the population, which had gradually increased to 20,000. By February 1942 about 18,000 men had died, including forty-six Germans who had caught the diseases. The prisoner of war camp was closed in the summer of 1942, and the few survivors were put to work as laborers in surrounding villages. The army installation remained.

In April 1943 the character of the camp changed when the German army turned part of it over to the S.S. (Schutzstaffel) to be used as a "transit camp" for Jews. (The S.S. was an elite group originally organized in the 1920s to protect the leaders of the Nazi party. It was in charge of the Gestapo, the secret police. Later the S.S. was entrusted with carrying out the so-called "Final Solution to the Jewish problem," namely the annihilation of Jews in the death camps. Members of the S.S. were armed and wore black uniforms to distinguish them from the run-of-the-mill S.A. stormtroopers, who wore brown uniforms.)

The camp was intended for Jews who held Latin-American passports, entry visas for Palestine, or were hostages. These Jews were supposed to be exchanged by the German government for Germans who had been interned by the Allies. About 9,000 Jews who met the criteria were transported from Poland, Greece, Holland, North Africa, France, Yugoslavia, and Hungary to Bergen-Belsen. About 3,200 of these were actually exchanged, while thousands were shipped out to extermination camps where they were murdered.

The camp had room for 10,000 inmates, but between December 1944 and March 1945 the population swelled rapidly as the Germans emptied other concentration camps in their retreat before the advancing Russians. The evacuees arrived after long forced marches and were starved and ill. Lack of food and of medical attention allowed epidemics to rage uncontrolled. In March 1945 alone more than 18,000 inmates died, including Anne Frank and her sister Margot.

When the British forces reached the entrance to the camp at 3:00 P.M. on April 15, 1945, they liberated about 58,000 inmates, the majority being women. For Anne and Margot Frank and the 13,000 who had died of weakness and disease within the first twelve weeks after liberation, the British forces had, unfortunately, arrived too late. On May 21 the Jews were moved from the camp to the quarters of the German army, and all the barracks of the camp were burned to the ground to prevent another typhus epidemic. At the end of May, 11,200 survivors remained in the military hospital where scores continued to die each day.

The British soldiers who had happened upon Bergen-Belsen were deeply shocked by the unbelievable horror they encountered. They sent reports and pictures to their families, and soon reporters arrived on the scene to record it on film. Bergen-Belsen became synonymous with piles of the 10,000 unburied corpses, the unbearable stench of diseased bodies and indescribable filth, and thousands of walking skeletons that had been totally dehumanized. As the smoking chimneys of the crematoria of Auschwitz came to symbolize the use of technology for mass murder, so the mountains of dead bodies at Bergen-Belsen came to represent the bestiality of which humans are capable.

It is to the eternal credit of the British officers that they immediately took action to involve former prison guards and local Germans in the burial of the dead and the care of the survivors. The civilian population of Bergen was forced to collect 2,000 woolen blankets; the mayors of nearby towns were required to assemble at the open trenches that served as mass graves; local newspapers carried explicit reports and gruesome photographs. The mayors responded as the May 23 appeal by the mayor of Hannover indicates. John's translation is printed below.

APPEAL FOR DONATIONS FOR
THE SURVIVORS OF BERGEN-BELSEN
ISSUED BY THE MAYOR OF HANNOVER
(Source: *New Hannover Courier*, June 5, 1945)

CITY OF HANNOVER
PROCLAMATION BY THE MAYOR

To the Residents of Hannover:

In the concentration camp Bergen-Belsen there are now about 20,000 former prisoners of the Nazi regime who have been so weakened through deprivation, torture, and disease that it will take at least six months before they can be transported out. In order to make life in the camp more bearable and pleasant for the unfortunate victims of criminal activity, I call upon the residents of Hannover to provide for them the following: books in all languages, except German, record players, phonograph records, musical instruments—ranging from string instruments to the piano—as well as board games such as checkers and chess. The donations should be taken to the appropriate local police district headquarters; or the police should be informed where these items can be picked up by properly identified authorized employees. In addition, donations will be collected from the donors' homes.

I am convinced that the citizens of Hannover, particularly those whose property was spared the ravages of war, will prove through their donations that they have nothing in common with the defeated Nazi regime, and that they are willing to help the unfortunate victims of this regime with all their available strength.

/s/ Hannover, May 23, 1945
Mayor of the Capital City of Hannover

On May 30, 1945, British Field Marshal Sir Bernard Montgomery informed the German people that he had been appointed by the British government to be in control of the area occupied by the British army. He promised that those who had committed war crimes would be dealt with in "proper fashion." In August, the Allies (the United States, Britain, France, and the Soviet Union) agreed to expand the legal basis for the prosecution of war criminals to include war crimes, crimes against humanity, and crimes against peace, enabling the courts to include atrocities against Jews, no matter what their nationality.

The first of the three Bergen-Belsen trials took place in Lüneburg. When the trial opened on September 17, 1945, it put Lüneburg on the international map. Overnight the tranquil old town became a bustling traffic center as reporters from all over the world filled the hotels. The ancient city square, Am Sande, was turned into a parking lot from which foreign correspondents shuttled back and forth to the huge gymnasium of the Men's Athletic Club, in which the trial took place. In 1976 Lüneburg razed the gymnasium in an effort to rid the town of this unwelcome reminder of the Nazi era.

The British made sure that the citizens of Lüneburg were informed of the reasons for the trial. Large photographs portraying mountains of the dead and the faces of the barely living of Bergen-Belsen were displayed in many store windows, and a special exhibit of drawings by a former camp inmate brought terrifying scenes of torture and murder to life. Among the citizens of Lüneburg an intense competition developed for tickets admitting observers to the trial.

The trial was a model of fairness. Each defendant was given the right to choose a lawyer for his defense, and while English was the language of the court, interpreters were provided for the German and Polish defendants. Since the British put on trial only those criminals who had been physically present and immediately arrested when the British forces arrived at the camp on April 15, there were only forty-four defendants in the dock. Exactly one day before the British take-over of the camp, the Nazis had "transferred" the majority of S.S. guards to another camp, and they effectively vanished. Moreover, seventeen of those arrested in April had since died of typhus.

On November 17 the court announced the verdict: Eight S.S. men and three S.S. women were condemned to death by hanging; nineteen received prison sentences, and fourteen were acquitted.

On December 12, 1945, the hangings took place at the penitentiary in Hameln, the old town of Hamelin of storybook fame.

The Second Bergen-Belsen Trial took place in Celle in May 1946, and the Third Bergen-Belsen Trial convened about two years later in Hamburg.

After the trials, the British began a search for the escaped S.S. guards. They succeeded in bringing a number of the criminals to justice, at first in British military courts and, after the withdrawal of the Allied occupation forces, in German courts. It goes without saying that those who disappeared vastly outnumbered those who were apprehended. There is no doubt that many of them eventually came out of hiding and reclaimed their positions in the German bureaucracy.

The story of Bergen-Belsen does not end here. For decades local newspapers would periodically report the discovery of unburied skeletons or mass graves on the site. Even the razing of the large gymnasium could not erase reminders of the past, and the people of Lüneburg would never be allowed to forget the reason for the Bergen-Belsen trials.

Dr. Erwin Lichtenstein surrounded by (left to right) Cousin Ruth, Aunt Lotte, Marion. Frankfurt, August 21, 1958.

Lüneburg: View from our hotel room window.

Embarkation in Bremerhaven.

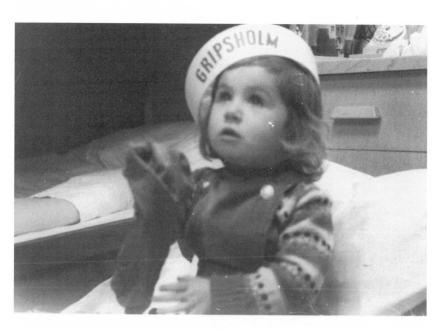

Above and below: Becky aboard the Gripsholm.

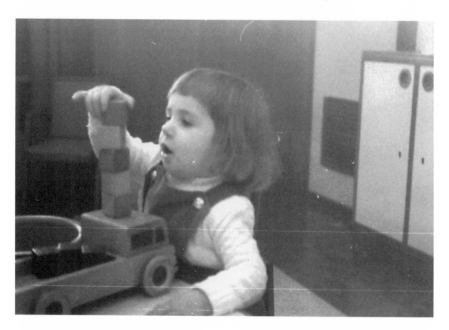

Becky and Marion aboard the Gripsholm.

John and Becky arrive in New York, November 6, 1958.
Note Püppi and hanky in Becky's hand.

Marion arrives in New York, November 6, 1958.

Marion and Becky at home in America.

XX

After a train ride of more than seven hours we arrived in Lüneburg. We had made a brief stop in Hannover to see Dr. Gold, our anchor, and to pick up a pile of letters that had accumulated. Dr. Gold seemed pleased to hear that we were moving to Lüneburg. "You will love that beautiful, ancient town," he said. "Architecturally it seems quite unchanged since medieval times. I don't recall that it was damaged during the war. The fourteenth-century Church of St. John and that of St. Nicholas, where J.S. Bach used to play the organ, have been maintained throughout the centuries and still offer weekly organ recitals." He smiled. "I realize that sightseeing is not your main objective," he said, "but you couldn't have picked a lovelier town for your search.

"You will need a lawyer sooner or later. My good friend Dr. König is the best attorney in town. Here is his address. Tell him I sent you," Dr. Gold added, as he handed John a card. "I'll be happy to keep your mail until you get settled. Keep in touch!"

The taxi driver dropped us off at a large hotel at the corner of Am Sande. A uniformed doorman helped us with our luggage and showed us to a high-ceilinged room on the second floor. "Look, John," I said, "this place is luxurious. Look at that huge tiled bathtub! I can't wait to use it."

We decided to have dinner in the restaurant downstairs. The menu was long, the portions were entirely too generous, and the prices were totally unreasonable. "I don't think we can afford to stay here," said John, shaking his head. "Let's enjoy the bathtub tonight," I pleaded. "Tomorrow we can move to a less expensive place."

As we returned to our room, we noticed a somewhat musty odor. Although it was drizzling outside, we opened the windows wide. John detected a couple of spiderwebs on top of the drapes. "Let me run the water," I called excitedly, as John began to unpack. "I can't get the faucets to budge. Could you please help me?"

John surveyed the situation. "They are frozen," he said after trying his best to loosen them. "I have a funny feeling that this room hasn't been used since the British officers left when the occupation ended," he mumbled. "Who can afford such prices anyway? Thank goodness, the toilet is working! Let's just wash up in the sink tonight and enjoy the clean towels. Good night!" And we crawled into bed.

The next morning, September 17, we moved to Hotel Stadt Hamburg, a few doors down on Am Sande. The cost of the room was less than half of what we had paid the night before, but there were no "luxuries." The room had a sink, but no hot water. A toilet was located down the hall, and once a week bath night was scheduled for the guests. "We are back in the Middle Ages," said John, "but at least the room is clean."

He opened the window. "What a lovely view," he said, "and we are practically next door to the Church of St. John! Let's stay here." And we did.

The letter from Lüneburg that we had received on September 13 had mentioned that two girls were available for adoption in the *Kinderheim* maintained by the county of Lüneburg. Past experience had taught us that it was the atmosphere of each individual orphanage and, especially, the educational philosophy of its director that determined the development of the children. It seemed like a good idea to visit the institution first to observe the children and then to begin the negotiations with the officials at the *Jugendamt*. We called the *Kinderheim*, referred to the letter, and were given an appointment to meet the director that afternoon.

Since the entire morning was free, we decided to explore the town. We stopped at the registration desk of the hotel and asked for directions to the important landmarks of Lüneburg. The owner showed us a map and pointed out the bus depot, train station, bank, shopping district, post office, and telephone building. In the summer Lüneburg attracts visitors to its spa and the lovely *Kurpark* (the gardens surrounding the baths) and to the ancient Lüneburg Heath; but now it was September and the hotels were almost empty. Mr. Schmidt, the owner of the hotel, was probably wondering what might cause two Americans to come to Lüneburg at this time of year.

"How long are you planning to stay here?" he inquired.

"We are here on business," John replied in a matter-of-fact voice, "and we can't predict yet how long our work will take."

"Let me know if I can be of service to you," said Mr. Schmidt as he bowed ever so slightly in our direction and handed us the timetables of the city buses and the intercity trains. In the weeks to come we would make good use of the schedules, but today we were going to see the neighborhood on foot.

As we were walking around in the center of town, window-shopping and admiring the old brick buildings, we noticed two British soldiers and a family of Danish tourists. Perhaps we were the only Americans in town. "I don't think we have any competition here," said John. We had heard that the British and Germans were not as interested in adopting children as the adoption-happy Americans who were overrunning the Frankfurt area.

We returned to our hotel for lunch in the wood-panelled dining room. The surroundings and the large, iron key to our room brought back memories of the Lion's Inn, where we had spent the night after meeting little Ulrich, but our spirits were different now. We were full of hope.

Kinderheim Am Bache (By the Brook) was located on the outskirts of Lüneburg. We walked for a good hour before spotting it in a wooded, park-like area. On our arrival we were greeted by the director, a nurse in a white uniform. She was slim and energetic. Her wavy brown hair was cut short, her face was expressive, and her greenish gray eyes betrayed curiosity as well as warmth. Somehow I felt that I had met her before.

Suddenly it occurred to me that she resembled my Aunt Paula, my father's only sister, whom I had adored as a child. It was Aunt Paula who had written into my autograph book "Always stand firm; never stand still!" The last time I had seen Aunt Paula had been at the train station in Berlin when my family left on a crowded refugee train for Holland. "Don't forget us!" she said as the train pulled out. She worked as a slave laborer in Berlin until the Nazis deported her to Auschwitz on February 27, 1943. It is believed that she was gassed immediately on the day that she arrived at the extermination camp.

And now I had the illusion that I had found her again in the

person of Ilse Heins! It was no wonder that I felt drawn to Miss
Heins, in whom I came to recognize the same keen intelligence, warm
sense of humor, and spirit of independence that I had admired in my
Aunt Paula.

Miss Heins ushered us into her office, and I noticed that she left
the door ajar. "Actually we have four adoptable children in the home
right now," she said. "I'll be happy to introduce them to you. However, I would like to know a bit about your own background and
your expectations. The better we get to know one another, the greater the chance of finding a child who would really fit into your family.
Human beings are so complex, and we want to be relatively certain
that the adoptive situation will bring happiness to the child as well as
to the parents."

There was a knock on the door. "Come on in," called Miss Heins.
A ruddy-cheeked boy of about five stood in the door. "I just wanted
to check if the door handle is working properly," he said earnestly.
"You know, I replaced the broken screw this morning."

"Thanks for checking! You are a good handyman," said Miss
Heins. "Now run along. The others are starting a soccer game in the
back yard!" They shook hands and the boy disappeared.

We continued our conversation. As we related the stories of our
lives in Europe and America, Miss Heins commented and asked questions. She then volunteered information about herself. She was a
trained nurse, and had been drafted during the war and sent to the
Russian front. She had seen more than her share of horrors and trag-
edies. When the war ended, she was happy to return to her main interest, children and their development. "There is more to consider
than just the physical health of the child," she explained. "I cannot
stand regimentation, and I firmly believe that it is possible to maintain discipline without insisting on blind, unquestioning obedience,"
she said.

She took us into a large room where the youngest children were
kept and pointed out Erika, a long, light blond child of five months.
"I think Erika will grow to be very tall. Frankly, I think she would
tower over both of you, and she is extremely fair. She is developing
very nicely, but I don't think she'd be suitable for you," Miss Heins
said.

We noticed that the cribs were not lined up in neat rows. Some were arranged at right angles to each other. "Over here is Paul. He is nine months old and beginning to stand. A local farm family has expressed an interest in him. You might want to check with the *Jugendamt* about his current status." We walked toward the crib of a plump, cherubic-looking girl. "Gisela is of Frisian background," said Miss Heins. "Her hair is very fine and so light that it seems almost white. Would you feel comfortable with her? She is almost ready to sit up. A very placid child," she added. "Konrad over here was born prematurely. He is beginning to catch up. I think he'd make a great truck driver, but I am not sure that he would fit into your family. What do you think?"

Miss Heins turned toward us. "If you go to the *Kreisjugendamt* (county youth office), you should also meet the social worker from the city youth office. The city maintains its own orphanage and may have adoptable children. It's worth a try.

"At any rate, please do come back tomorrow, if possible. I know of a little girl of twenty months who might be suitable for you. Because she is just getting over whooping cough, she is staying with a foster family in the country. When she gets well, she will return to the *Kinderheim*. You will come tomorrow, won't you?" Miss Heins pleaded. "This little girl is very special. I will need more time to tell you about her, but now I am needed by the children." A group of lively youngsters was coming in from the ball game. They crowded around Miss Heins.

"See you soon!" we called as we left.

XXI

The next morning we were awakened by a strange piercing sound. "I wonder where it comes from? It sounds very close," John said as he jumped out of bed and ran to the window. "It reminds me of a reveille in the army. It's exactly eight o'clock," he added. "Perhaps it's some kind of signal." And then the sound stopped. "Maybe we can solve this mystery tomorrow," I said.

There was a knock on the door. One of the cleaning women was bringing us a large kettle of hot water. What a godsend! By rationing it out, mixing some of it with the cold water in the sink, and saving the rest to brush our teeth, we could manage quite well. "If we stay in Lüneburg for any length of time, I'll have to think up some kind of housekeeping system. Eating all our meals out is going to run into money, and we really need to save," I was thinking out loud. From the window I could see the sign of a bakery across the street, and I remembered passing a grocery shop and a hardware store in one of the side streets that branched off Am Sande.

After a quick breakfast in the hotel dining room we walked briskly to the *Kreisjugendamt* to keep our appointment with Mr. Becker, the social worker, and Inspector Edel. When we arrived, we were greeted very cordially by both gentlemen. They already knew of our mission, for Miss Heins had informed them of our coming. The folder pertaining to Annie, the little girl who was quarantined with whooping cough, was on Mr. Edel's desk. "We have reviewed Annie's file carefully," said the inspector, "and, in general, the papers seem to be in order. The first step, of course, is for you to see the child at the foster home where she is presently staying. If you should decide to declare for Annie, we will help you in any way we possibly can.

"The next bus for Neustadt will leave at 1 P.M. I will notify the foster mother, Mrs. Brotmann, that you are coming. Mr. Becker can give you detailed instructions on how to find the house. I am looking forward to seeing you in my office at 10 A.M. tomorrow so that we can discuss the specific requirements for Annie's case." Mr. Edel impressed us as being efficient and friendly. We felt confident that he was on our side.

I realized that the tiny toy cars I carried in my purse might not be suitable for a little girl, and so we stopped at a toy store near the bus depot. I picked out a molded plastic doll, about six inches tall, with a painted Dutch boy haircut. It had sturdy legs and disproportionately wide shoes that enabled it to stand up securely. Although it was light-weight, it looked indestructible.

We bought round-trip tickets to Neustadt and boarded the bus. The handful of passengers seemed to be regulars. They probably had jobs in Lüneburg and were going home for the midday meal. After about fifteen minutes we stopped in Neustadt, a development of modest brick bungalows. The side streets were unpaved, and the large yards with fruit trees, compost piles, and a few stray chickens gave the area a rural flavor. We had no trouble finding the house of the Brotmanns where little Annie was staying.

Mrs. Brotmann was looking out for us and invited us in. She explained that the house was only three years old and that the devel-opment was among the first in the area to be connected to a sewer system. "At last we have a toilet inside the house," she said proudly, "and with the three children it is a great convenience." We inquired about Annie. "Oh, she is outside. She is getting over her whooping cough, and the doctor said she needed lots of fresh air. You must excuse her dirty face. She hates to have it washed, you know. She will avoid water whenever she can," Mrs. Brotmann chuckled.

We walked around the house, and there she was! Little Annie was playing contentedly on the compost pile. When she saw us, she pro-ceeded to stand on her head and then rolled down the pile, landing in front of our feet. "What a show-off," said John, observing Annie. She did look like a little scarecrow, with bits of straw in her hair, a thread-bare once-white tricot shirt and grayish overalls covered with a wrin-kled apron, and scuffed boots. "What a lucky kid!" I said. Fearlessly she approached John and reached for his hand, leading him to a small tree of purple plums. "Here," she said, *"Pflaumen"* (Plums).

Mrs. Brotmann arrived on the scene. "Annie," she said emphatically, "remember I told you *eine* (one only)!"

"*Eine,*" said Annie with an angelic smile, as she filled the pocket of her apron with a handful of plums. "*Eine und noch eine* (another one)," and she began to munch the fruit.

"We had better go inside now. Annie, you'll get sick if you eat another one," urged the foster mother. "Excuse us while we wash up," she said to us.

We returned to the house and sat down at the dining table. Annie came running in. "Uncle," she said as she climbed on John's lap. Her face and hands were sparkling clean, and her light brown hair was combed. We noticed that she had gray-brown eyes with long, dark eyelashes.

"Annie, I have something for you," I said and handed her the plastic doll.

"Ah, *Püppi,*" squealed the little girl, pressing the doll to her chest. She walked to the table. We watched her as she stood the doll on a napkin and very carefully pulled the napkin across the table, making sure the doll would not fall over. Annie repeated this "trick" several times. "*Müde*" (tired), she said. "*Püppi müde,*" and she lovingly covered the doll with the napkin. "*Püppi hei-a, hei-a*" (dolly night-night), she whispered, as if to remind the adults not to wake the doll. I watched John; he seemed spellbound.

Mrs. Brotmann explained that she was licensed as foster mother by the *Jugendamt* and that, in addition to Annie, she was taking care of a six-year-old boy and her own eleven-year-old daughter. She adored little Annie, and if it had not been for lack of money she would have liked to adopt her legally. We sensed that she dreaded having to part with the child. "I've had many little girls staying with me, but this one is different. She is so bright and she knows exactly what she wants. I am afraid I'm spoiling her rotten," she admitted, her eyes glistening. "It's time for Annie's nap. Please come back soon. If you come in the late afternoon next time, you can meet the other children, and we can have coffee and cake together." She handed me the doll. "Keep this for Annie. I wouldn't want anything to happen to it. Bring it along when you come back." Annie had wandered off into the garden. She was busy picking up plums from the ground and stuffing them into her apron.

We decided to hike the six miles back into town. The area around Lüneburg is entirely flat, perfect for bicycling and easy for walking. On a clear day we could cover distances that we would not even attempt back home in Washington.

Before returning to Hotel Stadt Hamburg we stopped in the bakery at Am Sande and bought three pieces of pastry and a bottle of mineral water for Friday's breakfast. "Why not invest in some kitchen items?" suggested John. At the hardware store around the corner we bought two mugs, three plates, two kitchen knives, several spoons, a can opener, and paper plates and napkins.

"You act as if we were going to stay in Lüneburg for a while," I teased John.

"Don't you agree that we should make this our home for the rest of our stay in Europe?" he replied. "Let's get a large immersion heater and a cooking pot. I hate to wash my hair in cold water," he said. "Tomorrow we'll go grocery shopping, and then we'll really set up housekeeping!"

We had dinner at the hotel. As we paid at the cash register, Mr. Schmidt mentioned that that night there would be an organ recital at St. John's Church. "I figured you would like music," he said.

I don't recall ever having attended an organ recital before, certainly not in a church built centuries ago. Knowing that J.S. Bach himself had played this organ made me appreciate the music even more. The huge edifice was, of course, unheated. The audience huddled in coats and scarves as they listened to the program of Bach and Schumann compositions. Occasionally people would glance in our direction, but to our surprise nobody stopped to ask if we were *Ausländer!* We looked at a bulletin board that listed future concerts, and John recorded the dates in his little leather diary. We agreed that this had been a great ending to a good day, and we were looking forward to tomorrow.

XXII

In anticipation of a busy day we rose early to enjoy our "picnic" breakfast in our hotel room. The pastries and mineral water hit the spot, and thanks to the immersion heater we had enough hot water to wash up and brush our teeth. "Tomorrow we'll enjoy a more balanced meal," I thought as I wrote out a shopping list.

And then we heard that piercing sound again! "It's exactly eight o'clock," said John, checking his watch.

We opened the window. "John, come quickly," I called excitedly. "I think I've discovered where the sound comes from!" I pointed to the tower of St. John's Church. "Look at that window! Do you see something sticking out of it?"

"No kidding! It's a bugle, and it's being blown by a real live bugler! This is amazing!" said John breathlessly. And then the sound stopped. The instrument disappeared inside the window. "I wonder for how many centuries Lüneburgers have risen to the sound of a bugle," John commented. "What a charming custom!"

We arrived at Inspector Edel's office at the appointed time and found him ready for us. "Little Erika, the blond five-month-old whom you met on Wednesday, has been promised to a family from out of town. She is no longer available," he said. "However, I understand that there are two little boys, both fourteen months old, free for adoption at the city orphanage. The social worker at the *Stadt Jugendamt* can inform you of the particulars when you stop at her office." John mentioned that we had visited Annie at her foster home. "I thought you might like her," said the inspector, "but it may be a bit too early to make a firm commitment. I suggest you see all the adoptable children in this area before you make a decision, a very important decision, indeed," he said in a serious tone. "Please do keep in touch with me." He rose to shake hands with us.

We stopped at the *Stadt Jugendamt* and were given the address of the city orphanage where Hans and Horst were staying. When we arrived at the building, in an old downtown area, we found that it was being renovated. It was surrounded by scaffolding, and workmen were busy with hammers and blowtorches. The noise was deafening. We climbed the stairs to the second floor and were shown to the boys' rooms. Hans was standing in his crib. He was fully dressed and wore tightly laced leather boots. There were three cribs in the room. When the children saw us they broke into screams loud enough to drown out the pounding and hammering. Their faces were full of terror and tears were running down their cheeks.

We had not expected such a reaction. "I guess this is better than being ignored," John muttered.

"Don't be upset," said the young woman who accompanied us. "The children probably thought that we had come to transfer them again. You see, with this renovation going on, we have to move them frequently, and that's why they are wearing their boots in bed," she explained. Hans was beginning to calm down, and I handed him a toy car that I had pulled out of my purse. He looked at it and began banging it against the crib rails. "Auto," I said. There was no response.

"Perhaps you can let us see Horst," I suggested, as I picked up the little car that Hans had flung over the rails. We walked down the hall, stood in the door of the room containing Horst, and were greeted with a chorus of screams and wails. Horst reached for the car and immediately threw it across the room. "I'm afraid we've come at a bad time," I said to the young woman. "Thank you for letting us see the boys." We signed the register at the desk and stepped out on the sidewalk.

"Let's go to see Miss Heins," I begged John. "This was a terribly depressing place. I wonder what they have experienced that makes them so fearful of strangers?" I couldn't wait to visit the spacious grounds and feel the fresh air of Kinderheim Am Bache. We called Miss Heins and agreed to visit her in the afternoon.

It was naptime when we arrived at the *Kinderheim*. Miss Heins looked pleased to see us. "Tell me your impressions of Annie," she said, leaning back in her chair. "Was she still coughing a lot?" We reported our observations, and Miss Heins nodded in agreement. "I think you sized Annie up quite accurately," she said. "She will not be an easy child to raise. You will have to set definite limits, but within these limits she should be free to develop at her own pace. She is very bright. From what you have told me about your own hopes and aspirations, I feel certain you could provide her with all the opportunities she deserves."

Miss Heins offered us a glass of lemonade. "Annie has been with us for about a year. Before she came to us, she had been in another home and possibly some foster homes. But as soon as she arrived here, she asserted herself. You could describe her as a born leader, or, if you will, a rather bossy little girl. No matter what the activity, she was always the first, and the other children would follow her lead. She began to talk very early."

"Oh, yes, I noticed that," I interjected. "We were quite impressed by her vocabulary."

"She is completely toilet trained," continued Miss Heins. "Trained is really not the proper word. She actually 'trained' herself. Would you believe that Annie refused to be spoonfed? The other children seemed quite content to eat their cereal and applesauce, mashed potatoes, or rice from a spoon held by an aide. But not Annie! She fussed so much that we finally gave in and prepared sandwiches for her!" Miss Heins laughed. "I am sure that is contrary to all the regulations in the book. Now Annie seems to be perfectly happy munching cheese or liverwurst sandwiches. We decided at a staff meeting that there was no point in holding her back."

Miss Heins rose, went to a bookshelf, and returned with a slim volume, *The Lüneburg Heath*. She handed us the book. "Have you ever visited the heath?" she asked. "No, we haven't," I replied, "but I remember poems and songs about the heath that I learned in elementary school." I began to hum one of my favorite tunes. Miss Heins added her voice. "It used to be an idyllic place when the heather was in bloom and large herds of sheep would graze there," she said rather wistfully. "That was all changed before and during the war, when the German army used the area for its maneuvers. Did you know that a horrible concentration camp was located near Bergen? That's about an hour from here. Anne Frank died there. She has become a heroine to young Germans who make pilgrimages to

Bergen-Belsen to honor her memory. Actually there is little to see there because the camp was burned down. Perhaps you might be interested in going there?" she asked, searching our faces. We did not respond.

In spite of the fact that ten close relatives of John had died there, or possibly because of that, we could not bring ourselves to visit the site. John had shown me photos of his cousins, aunts, and uncles who had fled to Holland from Germany only to be rounded up by the Nazis after Holland's occupation. One of his favorite cousins had looked very much like Anne Frank. After a long silence I heard myself say, "We don't need reminders. They are always on our minds. Nothing will bring them back to life."

Miss Heins looked at us sadly. Again she reminded me of my Aunt Paula. "It must be so difficult for you to be back in Germany," she said softly.

"We like Lüneburg," said John. "Everyone here has been very helpful to us. May we come back on Monday? We would like to learn more about Annie, if you can spare the time."

"Certainly," said Miss Heins.

XXIII

On the way back to the hotel we stopped at several small stores (supermarkets were not yet known in Lüneburg) to buy groceries, baked goods, and fresh fruit. The greengrocer provided a wooden crate to serve as pantry for the bouillon cubes, bread, eggs, end pieces of liverwurst, chunks of cheese, mustard, cookies, apples, and carrots that we bought. Instant coffee, powdered hot chocolate, assorted teas, and packages of dry soup mixes would be arranged in a shoebox on the wide windowsill. Since there was no refrigeration available, we bought "milk in a tube" and a small can of condensed milk for our breakfast coffee. Dishtowels served as tablecloths. Of necessity I learned to create recipes for use with an electric immersion heater, and soon we were enjoying such delicacies as poached eggs, bouillon cube-noodle soup, hot dogs, and various cooked vegetables. John suggested I should write a book on "immersion heater hotel room cookery," but I didn't think that a market for such a publication existed. As for us, we would reduce our expenses substantially by eating out only once a day.

We had almost forgotten that Friday was "bath night" at the hotel, but Mr. Schmidt reminded us to sign up so that we would be guaranteed sufficient hot water. There were two bathrooms (in the true sense of the word) on our floor. Each contained a large enameled tub, a functional fixed shower, and a large water tank heated by briquets of coal. There was a wooden bench, several hooks for clothes or bathrobes, and a basket for used towels. An attendant handed the bather a huge, fluffy towel and a washcloth, while we provided our own soap.

For us the weekly bath took on the importance of a quasi-religious ceremony. Its fragrant mist provided a half-hour of total relaxation and marked the end of a hectic work week. We returned to our room refreshed, ready to plan the weekend.

The next morning we took the train to Hannover. The time had come to collect our mail and to inform Dr. Gold that we were making Lüneburg our official headquarters, to which all letters should be forwarded. We had prepared a large manila envelope for that purpose. When we reported on the progress of our search we were reminded by Dr. Gold of the legal obstacles we would have to overcome to be able to adopt Annie and take her with us to America. "Call me if you think I can be of any help," he said. "We will keep you informed," we assured him as we left.

We realized that this visit to Hannover would probably be our last. Once more we walked around the lively city, had dinner in an outdoor restaurant, and recalled that our search had begun in this town. "I wonder how Anton is getting along," I thought. It was barely five weeks ago that we had met him, and yet it seemed as if years had passed.

The trains were running on a weekend schedule and we had time to spare. John used the opportunity to call Erwin Lichtenstein, our anchor in Frankfurt, to tell him that we would stay in Lüneburg "for the duration."

"I have a letter for you," said Erwin. "It is from Mr. Schneider in Giessen and might be important. Would you like me to open it?" he asked. He began to read "Enclosed is the letter from Mrs. O'Neill of the county social service office. Please notice that it is sealed. It must not be opened by anyone other than the inspector of the *Jugendamt* who serves as legal guardian of the child you are planning to adopt. The letter contains the report of the home study required by your county, and I am delighted to tell you that it is very favorable. With this document you have satisfied the American as well as the German adoption requirements. Congratulations!"

"That's fantastic," gasped John. "Please forward Mr. Schneider's letter right away. This document will arrive just in time! On second thought, please send it to us by *registered* mail. It is extremely important!"

"This is what I call progress!" John said as he turned to me, beaming. "I'll tell you all about it on the train."

On Sunday we awoke to brilliant sunshine. What a perfect day to explore Lüneburg! We walked around the town looking for traces of the existence of a Jewish community. In vain we had searched the telephone book for Jewish names. Yom Kippur (Day of Atonement), the most sacred day in the Jewish calendar, would be observed on Tuesday, and I realized that for the first time in my life I would not be attending the day-long service in a synagogue. For a fleeting moment I considered returning to the U.S. Army base in Frankfurt to join the soldiers in prayer, but I quickly dismissed that thought. The process of adopting Annie had to be our top priority.

In conversations with Miss Heins and other Lüneburgers we learned that there were no Jews left in Lüneburg. The stately synagogue with its beautiful dome had been one of the landmarks of the town. It had been endowed by Marcus Heineman, a prominent Jewish citizen of Lüneburg, and was dedicated in 1894 with a special prayer for the health of the Kaiser. In those days, there were 130 Jews in Lüneburg. The synagogue seated 200 persons and served the community until November 1938, when it was demolished.

There is evidence that a Jewish presence in Lüneburg goes back to 1288. Like other Jewish settlements in Germany, the one in Lüneburg suffered the usual persecutions and expulsions throughout the centuries, and by 1845 a "permanent" community of forty persons was recorded. The Jewish population reached its peak of 175 individuals in 1905, partly as the result of the influx of immigrants who had fled the Russian pogroms and had found refuge in Lüneburg. When Hitler seized power in 1933, the population shrank to 114, and in October 1939 only 16 were still in Lüneburg. All 16 were deported to extermination camps in 1943.

Although Jews never exceeded one third of one percent of the total population, their presence was felt in the public life of Lüneburg. Aside from the majestic synagogue building on the banks of the Ilmenau, the city's largest department store, a shoe store, drygoods store, and the offices of lawyers, a doctor, and a dentist testified to the fact that the Jews of Lüneburg were solid local citizens. After 1933 they shared the fate of all German Jews. Almost overnight they lost their livelihoods, their possessions, and became social outcasts. The mayor, who had been installed by the Nazi party at age twenty-eight, seemed to have been an anti-Semite of the first order. Shortly before the end of the war many documents relating to the history and fate of the Jewish community were systematically destroyed, a practice that continued into the seventies.

After the liberation of Bergen-Belsen a group of survivors of the camp were temporarily housed in Lüneburg. Most of them emigrated to Israel.

In 1987 a group of dedicated volunteers established the Historical Workshop of Lüneburg, whose aim it is to study and document how the historical events of the past seventy-five years have been reflected in the local history of Lüneburg. The research of the workshop has resulted in a number of publications, among them *Jüdische Familien in Lüneburg: Erinnerungen* (*Jewish Families in Lüneburg: Memories*) and *Lüneburg unter dem Hakenkreuz* (*Lüneburg under the Swastika*), both published in 1995. These books, richly illustrated with photographs and carefully documented, provided the basis of the information in this chapter. At the time of my writing this book (1997) I was in active correspondence with several members of the Historical Workshop, courageous women who have made it their mission to inform their countrymen of the horrors of the Nazi regime and of the fate of their Jewish neighbors.

XXIV

We began the next week with a visit to Miss Heins. She was anxious to see us, for another little boy had just become available for adoption. As we entered the room, he greeted us with a smile. Perhaps he remembered us from our past visits? As Miss Heins began to tell us about him, I realized that I had difficulty concentrating on her words. It seemed that on a subconscious level my mind had already chosen Annie. For a moment I thought it would be ideal to adopt two children at the same time. But even if it had been legally feasible, we lacked the financial resources for such a bold undertaking.

Apparently John had been thinking along similar lines. "Since we can take only one child, we will have to narrow our choice. Of all the children we have seen, we have been most impressed by Annie," he said slowly and deliberately. "She already has a distinct personality. Don't you think she is rather special?" he asked Miss Heins.

We followed Miss Heins into her office. "Annie certainly knows what she wants and how to get it," she said smilingly, "but she also adapts easily to new situations. Mrs. Brotmann, the foster mother with whom Annie has been staying for almost a month, has nothing but praise for her. Since she has cared for many babies and toddlers, I tend to trust her judgment. You may also consult Mrs. Mann, the caseworker who has known Annie ever since her mother made the decision to give her up."

Miss Heins was called out of the office by one of her assistants. When she returned we resumed the conversation. "Lüneburg is a small town, you know," she said. "People like to gossip, especially when few facts are known, as is the case with Annie. You can imagine the frustration of the curious townspeople!" She paused. "I would be so happy to see Annie placed with a loving, responsible couple," she said.

"What would happen to Annie if she were *not* adopted?" I wanted to know. "Would she have any opportunity to get a good education?"

"Most children from the orphanages attend the *Volksschule*; that is, they study the basic subjects for eight years. The boys usually receive some technical training after that and then serve an apprenticeship for a trade. Girls often take jobs in households and later work in places like the restaurants in the railroad stations."

"Do any of these young people ever go to a university?" John asked.

"I doubt it," said Miss Heins, shaking her head. "In general, the opportunities are quite limited. That is just one reason why I am always eager to help find families for my children. I do believe that everyone has latent talents. Unfortunately, few orphans are given the chance to develop them," she said seriously. "Let me know when you arrive at a decision."

We left the *Kinderheim* and walked to the *Kurgarten*. We found a bench on the main path.

"What are we going to do?" I asked.

"Well," said John, "we have an appointment tomorrow with Inspector Edel. Let's declare for Annie. If for some reason we can't have *her*, let's call off the search."

"I feel that Annie was meant for us," I said, and John nodded.

We took the bus into town. John made arrangements to rent a typewriter and a radio. "We'll need both of them, I am sure," he said.

On Tuesday morning, as we were leaving for our appointment at the *Kreisjugendamt*, Mr. Schmidt stopped us. "Yesterday morning the mailman said he had a registered letter for you. Your signature was needed, but you were out. He promised to come back early today," he said as he stepped out the door. "I see him across the street! He'll be here in just a few minutes!"

As we had guessed, it was the letter that Erwin had forwarded to us. We opened it and read Mr. Schneider's lines but left the enclosed report from Mrs. O'Neill untouched as had been requested. "Good timing," said John. "We have won the first skirmish of the paper war!"

Mrs. Mann, Annie's caseworker, joined us for the conference with

Inspector Edel. She spoke in favor of our taking Annie and offered her services in case they were needed in the future. Inspector Edel concurred. We handed him the sealed envelope from Mrs. O'Neill. Without opening it, he filed it in the folder marked "Family Wolff," and then he turned to us.

"Since you will have to satisfy the immigration laws for the child, I would suggest that you visit the U.S. consulate in Hamburg to obtain a copy of the requirements. I will be glad to assist you and your lawyer in guiding your application through the various steps with the police, health department, and the guardianship court," he offered.

"I understand that the U.S. consulate requires a thorough physical examination of all prospective immigrants," John remarked. "Since we know nothing of Annie's background, we were wondering if Annie could be admitted to the Children's Hospital in Hamburg for some tests and observation. We imagine that such an examination might also satisfy the American requirements."

"This sounds like a good idea, but you need to check it out with the American authorities. When are you planning to visit the consulate?" asked Mr. Edel.

"On the next train," I said. "We have no time to lose!"

We arrived in Hamburg in the early afternoon and made our way to the consulate. The office staff did not seem overly busy, and we were able to meet with the vice consul himself. He handed us the printed instructions (see below), discussed each point with us, and complimented us on having qualified as adopters in our home state. As to the medical examination, he indicated that while the decision was up to the U.S. Public Health Service doctor, he himself did not foresee any problems. "Of course, the child needs to be vaccinated against smallpox before an immigration visa can be issued," he reminded us.

At the U.S. consulate in Hamburg, we were given a set of instructions dated March 14, 1958, summarized below.

ADOPTION OF CHILDREN IN GERMANY

Adoptions in Germany involve the following three steps:

1. The adopting parents and the legal representative of the child conclude a contract before a German court or notary public. The adopting parents will be required to submit a certified copy of their marriage license, their passports, and medical certificates to indicate that they are in good health. It may also be helpful to have letters of reference and other documents. Before undertaking this step, *the adopting parents should also be prepared to prove that they qualify as adopters under the law of their home state.* It has been noted that an *excerpt from* Martindale-Hubbell's Law Directory *may be sufficient as proof of the law of the adopter's home state.*

2. Next, the following consents to the adoption are obtained:
(a) The consent of the child when older than 14 years.
(b) The consent of the child's parents—or, in the case of an illegitimate child, the consent of the mother—if the child is under 21 years of age. This consent must be of an irrevocable nature and must be declared before a notary public.
(c) The consent of the guardian when the parent is not the child's legal representative. When the child is illegitimate, the youth office generally is the legal representative and normally concludes the adoption contract.
(d) The consent of the Guardianship Court (*Vormundschaftsgericht*). Before giving its consent, the Guardianship Court must consult the local youth office.

3. Finally, the adoption contract must be confirmed before a local court. Without this confirmation the adoption has not been concluded and is not effective. While there has been some doubt whether a German court can act when the adoptive parents have neither residence nor abode in Germany, *the prevailing view is affirmative.*

Once the adoption decree has been issued, it is possible to *change the child's surname to that of the adoptive parents.* Application for change of Christian name is made to the chief of police of the district where the child is registered. When the change of name is completed, it is possible to obtain an amended birth certificate which gives the child's new name and the names of the adoptive parents. On the basis of this amended birth certificate a passport and immigration visa can be issued in the child's new name.

Adopted children who are not American citizens will require visas for admission to the United States. Assuming that the child is a German quota national (i.e., was born in the German quota area as constituted in the Immigration and Nationality Act of 1952, which embraces the territories within the 1938 boundaries of Germany), there should be little delay between filing an application and receiving a visa. Actual procedures will depend on circumstances at the time and will be explained by the visa-issuing office. It is necessary for a *child to undergo a medical examination by a U.S. Public Health Service Doctor* prior to the issuance of an immigration visa.

He gave John several forms, including one for the required affidavit of support (guarantee that sufficient funds were available so that the new immigrant would not become a "public charge") and another to apply for a visa. "The application for a visa cannot be submitted until *after* the German court has *ratified* the formal adoption," the vice consul emphasized.

"The typewriter will come in very handy," said John, contemplating the future challenges of the paper war.

XXV

W hat makes the waging of a paper war so nerve-wracking is the uneven speed of its course. The tempo alternates between frantic efforts to meet successive deadlines and periods of uneventful waiting. One never knows for sure if one's efforts have been productive and, since one cannot initiate the next step in the chain of formalities without the successful completion of the preceding link, one is left in a perpetual state of tension. By necessity we became expert jugglers of time, train schedules, appointments, and finances.

Inspector Edel of the county *Jugendamt* went out of his way to be helpful. He approved our request to have Annie undergo a thorough physical examination and made the arrangements with Professor Montag of the Children's Hospital in Hamburg to have Annie admitted. Mr. Edel explained the legal requirements to us, assuming all along that Annie would be found to be in good health and able to withstand the voyage across the ocean.

In the afternoon we met our lawyer, Dr. König. His office was located within easy walking distance from our hotel and, as time went on, it became a second home for us, or so it seemed. The office was staffed by three secretaries who used manual typewriters to prepare the documents with incredible speed and amazing accuracy. Miss Long, the typist assigned to our case, was a model of courtesy and efficiency; there were many afternoons when she worked overtime to process the papers required by the guardianship court.

With the guidance of Dr. König, John drew up a flow chart of all the hurdles that needed to be overcome by October 29, the scheduled day of our departure from Germany. (The chart appears on the following page.)

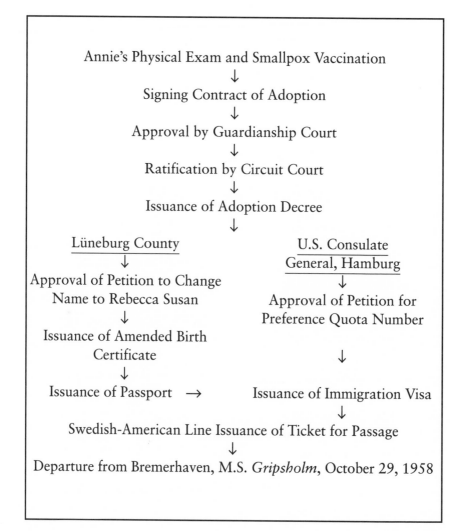

Annie's Physical Exam and Smallpox Vaccination
↓
Signing Contract of Adoption
↓
Approval by Guardianship Court
↓
Ratification by Circuit Court
↓
Issuance of Adoption Decree
↓

Lüneburg County   U.S. Consulate
↓   General, Hamburg
Approval of Petition to Change   ↓
Name to Rebecca Susan   Approval of Petition for
↓   Preference Quota Number
Issuance of Amended Birth
Certificate   ↓
↓
Issuance of Passport →   Issuance of Immigration Visa
↓
Swedish-American Line Issuance of Ticket for Passage
↓
Departure from Bremerhaven, M.S. *Gripsholm*, October 29, 1958

The German language we had spoken as children had not prepared us to deal with the legal jargon in which the documents were written. John would spend hours at the typewriter, dictionary at hand, composing letters, applications, and petitions to various agencies, and translating these documents from one language to the other. Before long he had become familiar with the legal vocabulary and was able to negotiate with the officials. His calm manner and thorough understanding of the legal maneuvers, down to minute details, impressed the German as well as the American bureaucrats. He was well on his way to qualifying as a lawyer!

At 7 A.M. on September 27, a social worker from the *Jugendamt* called for John. Together they drove out to Neustadt to pick up Annie and reach the station in time for the 7:40 train to Hamburg. While Annie was being admitted to the children's division of the University Hospital, John had an interview with Professor Montag, head of the pediatrics department. Apparently Dr. Montag was somewhat perplexed by our wish to have Annie admitted. After all, except for the whooping cough, she seemed perfectly fine according to the records of the county health department. Moreover, German doctors were not as inclined to trust test results as readily as their American colleagues. Why did we want to adopt Annie in the first place? And who would pay for the procedures? Clearly, explanations were needed. It definitely worked to John's advantage that as a biochemist, he could talk to Dr. Montag in scientific medical terms (rather than in his recently acquired legalese) in order to enlist the pediatrician's cooperation. Together they made a list of tests appropriate for Annie. Dr. Montag promised to see us on September 30 to discuss the test results with us and to have Annie discharged.

The next day we took the train to Hamburg to visit Annie. We found her in a large, airy room on the isolation ward. It must have been a lonely time for her, and she was delighted to see us. *"Pielen,"* (*spielen*—play) she begged us. We had brought along a bag of brightly colored wooden building blocks and scattered them on a table. Then we observed Annie, who proceeded to balance the blocks one on top of the other. She was totally focused as she built a tower; her mouth was open, and the pinky of her right hand was raised daintily as she put each block in its proper place. And when the tower collapsed, she started all over, chuckling with delight.

A young nurse came into the room. She told us that Annie had already become the darling of the pediatric floor. "What kind of diapers does Annie use at night?" I inquired. The nurse stared at me in surprise. "Annie doesn't use any diapers! She is completely toilet trained! We pick her up once and put her on the potty. That's around 11 P.M., and Annie sleeps through it all. She is such a darling! The doctor told me she is not afraid of anything, and that is quite unusual."

The next day we again visited Annie, who seemed to be expecting us. *"Steinchen,"* (little blocks) she demanded as she saw us coming, and again we watched her construct towers and walls methodically and patiently. When we left her we assured her that we would come back tomorrow.

We took a guided bus tour through the city of Hamburg, a truly impressive harbor town, before returning to Lüneburg.

On September 30 we visited Annie briefly and then kept our appointment with Dr. Montag, while the social worker arranged for Annie's discharge. The doctor told us that Annie seemed completely healthy in mind and body. The chest x-ray still showed "streaks" in her lungs, but that was to be expected after her bout with whooping cough. As to her mental development, every question on the lengthy form had been answered by "age-appropriate," a rather vague appraisal. One part of the "test" had consisted of taking Annie on a walk on the hospital grounds and having her point out objects such as trees, flowers, pebbles, and birds. To the examiner's surprise Annie had stopped to wave to a passing airplane, describing it appropriately by the word *"Flieger."* This episode was noted in the record. Dr. Montag said that it indicated "above average" alertness. We were relieved to hear that the results of all the laboratory tests were "within normal limits" and that Annie was ready to be discharged.

The four of us had lunch in the station restaurant, and then we boarded the train to Lüneburg. Annie fell asleep on the lap of the social worker. It had been a big day for a little girl!

XXVI

The next morning we met Annie at the health department clinic. Mrs. Brotmann, the foster mother, had come by bicycle, her usual mode of travel, with Annie securely strapped in the baby seat in the back. Every seat in the waiting room was taken, and a handful of patients were standing in the hall. We suggested to Mrs. Brotmann that she might want to spend an hour shopping while we took care of Annie. She gladly accepted our offer. At last, John found a seat. He kept Annie amused by bouncing her on his knees and reciting *"Hoppe, hoppe, Reiter"* (Hop, hop, rider) in a rhythmic monotone. I spied a seat across the room and sat down. I looked around the room and noticed two women whispering and turning their heads toward John.

An assistant appeared and called Annie's name. John stood up, gathering her in his arms. "So *that's* the child's father," one of the women whispered audibly as she pointed in John's direction. "Yes, I *am* the child's father," John announced firmly. The women fell silent as John and Annie followed the assistant. "What a perfect way to squelch all the rumors," I thought. And then I heard someone call *my* name.

A man in a white coat asked me to step into a cubicle. "Please undress and put this on," he ordered, handing me a flimsy hospital gown. I sat down on the wooden seat, studied the hooks on the wall, and felt the blood rushing to my face. I decided not to undress. There was absolutely no reason why I needed to be examined by this German doctor. I had familiarized myself with the German adoption laws before we had left America, and I knew that they required proof that the adoptive mother was unable to have biological children, but was healthy in all other respects. Two well-known infertility specialists had examined me and, on the basis of exhaustive tests, had documented my condition. John had translated their testimonies into German, and an American notary had put his seal on them.

This was not the first time a German official had ordered me to undress. It had happened before, on November 15, 1939, when I was separated from my family for the strip search, one of the crucial tests the Nazis inflicted on the frightened refugees before permitting them to cross the border into Holland. I was fourteen at the time. The feelings of humiliation, helplessness, and terror I experienced as the woman attendant checked for contraband in clothes, shoes, and between my toes have never left me. I had heard that some refugees had been arrested on trumped-up charges, and I was terribly worried that something might happen to my parents and my sister. But that was 1939, and I was a stateless Jewish refugee; now it was 1958, and I was a proud American citizen. I no longer felt helpless.

The doctor knocked on the folding door of the cubicle and inquired whether I was ready to come out. I opened the door. "There is no need for this examination," I said firmly. "My health reports have been submitted to the *Jugendamt*. If you have any questions, you may consult Inspector Edel or my lawyer." The doctor looked dumbfounded and retreated.

I returned to the waiting room, and sat down. Soon John and Annie reappeared. The report from Dr. Montag had been accepted by the clinic as satisfying the requirements for a health certificate. Annie had been vaccinated against smallpox, as required by the U.S. State Department. In one week she was to return to have the vaccination read so that John could apply for the American visa.

Mrs. Brotmann returned just in time to claim Annie. She tied a red kerchief around the little girl's head, strapped her into the bicycle seat, and rode off in the direction of Neustadt. Annie looked back and waved to us.

John and I had a great deal to talk about. We decided to celebrate by going to a restaurant known for a Lüneburg specialty, savoy cabbage and *Schnucken* (the moor sheep that grazed on the Lüneburg heath are known as *Schnucken*). The meal cost more than we had budgeted, but this day had been special. We had made great progress in our quest, and we had reason to be proud of each other.

We spent the afternoon in Inspector Edel's office preparing the documents that were needed for the signing of the contract of adoption. The conclusion of this contract must take place before a notary public and constitutes the first legal step in the adoption procedure. It was our good fortune that Dr. König, our lawyer, was qualified not only to guide us through the legal maze but also to serve as notary public.

Our file, bulging with letters and documents, was lying open on Inspector Edel's table. He had made a list of all the requirements: a certified copy of our marriage license, medical records for both of us, evidence that we had qualified as adopters under the laws of the State of Maryland (Mrs. O'Neill's letter), certified copies of our passports, and many letters of reference. The *Jugendamt* of the county of Lüneburg provided the child's official health certificate, which we had obtained only that morning. Inspector Edel also had proof that he, as head of the *Jugendamt*, served as the child's guardian and her legal representative.

Mr. Edel, John, and I examined the papers, making sure that each had been properly signed and notarized. The inspector then checked off every item on the master list, noting which documents were available in the original and in translation. "I am really impressed," he said. "You certainly have prepared your case well. I can't think of anything else the court could possibly need." We heaved a sigh of relief. "On Friday afternoon at three o'clock we will meet in Dr. König's office for the formal signing of the adoption contract. See you there," he said, and he rose to shake hands with us.

"This has been quite a day," John said as we walked to the hotel. "I'm worn out," I admitted. "Let's stop at the bakery for dessert and tomorrow's breakfast. I'll fix soup and sandwiches in our room. It's all right with me if I don't see any official papers for a while."

John nodded in agreement. "Wouldn't it be nice if there would be a concert on the radio tonight? A Mozart program, for example, would definitely revive me!" he said with a smile.

XXVII

When we arrived at Dr. König's office on Friday afternoon, we had no idea that the examination and notarization of our documents would take nearly three hours. At last, at six o'clock, all of the papers had been approved and the contract of adoption was duly signed by Inspector Edel, Annie's legal guardian, and by us, the prospective adoptive parents. We realized the importance of this step, the first in a long chain of legal hurdles that had to be overcome in order to transform our dream into reality.

"This is the time to file the application for change of name with the county office," Dr. König reminded us. He handed John the required form. "However, final approval of the petition for the name change cannot be granted until the decree of adoption has been issued, and that depends on the action of the guardianship court and the circuit court. There is, of course, no guarantee that the judge will approve the contract of adoption that you signed. You realize that the time limit you have set requires special handling of your case." He paused to consult with Mr. Edel on how to proceed from here.

The inspector sat down next to us. "There are two judges in the county who could take your case," he said in a low voice. "Dr. König and I have agreed to ask Judge Tremel if he can fit you into his schedule as soon as possible. Judge Tremel is a very fine person and competent jurist, and we trust that he will give you a fair hearing." Mr. Edel promised to let us know when we were to appear in court. "I will make certain that the fifteen legal documents and the notarized contract of adoption are on the judge's desk on Monday," Dr. König assured us. "Remember to complete the change of name form before you leave the office," he repeated.

Choosing a name for a child is not an easy matter. A "given" name not only serves as identification for the rest of your life, but also evokes very subjective associations. For me, for example, "Shirley" means curls and dimples; "Gretchen" belongs in Goethe's drama *Faust*; "Rachel" brings to mind a graceful maiden with long, black hair; and "Victoria" or "Elizabeth" suggest royalty or, at least, nobility. I soon found out that John did not share my fantasies and biases. In fact, he thought my ideas were downright silly. What mattered to him was the musical ring of the name, a pleasant cadence of sounds that harmonized with the last (family) name. In our case, "Wolff" almost demanded a first name of three syllables. We agreed that we wanted a biblical name, one that had passed the test of time, yet was neither old fashioned nor trendy. "Rebecca" seemed to meet all of these qualifications, including the connotation of the biblical Rebecca, a kind and caring person.

John completed the change of name application by inserting "Rebecca Susan Wolff" in the appropriate space. "We can start out by calling her Becky," he said as he handed the form to the secretary. Again Miss Long had agreed to stay overtime to help us. We felt a bit guilty when we left the office while she was still typing. But tonight was bath night at our hotel, and we were anxious not to miss our turns.

On Saturday we visited Annie at the Brotmanns' in Neustadt. Despite a slightly swollen arm, the result of the vaccination, Annie was her usual bubbly self. We felt that she no longer considered us strangers. She reached for John's hand and led him outside to her favorite plum tree. "*Here, eine*" (one) she said as she picked the fruit off the low-hanging branches to hand to him. Mrs. Brotmann appeared at the door. "Annie!" she called, "no more plums for you! I've set the table inside. Come!" She turned to us. "Annie just loves home-baked chocolate cake."

At the mention of the magic word Annie dashed inside. All of us washed our hands and joined the rest of the family around the table. There were Herr and Frau Brotmann, their eleven-year-old daughter, Betty, and a six-year-old foster son. The girl was shy and well mannered, while the boy had to make a great effort to sit still long enough to eat his slice of cake. As we had come to expect, Annie was in control of the situation. "*Lade Kuchen*," (chocolate cake) she demanded impatiently, pushing her plate towards Mrs. Brotmann. "Annie hasn't learned yet to wait her turn," said the foster mother apologetically.

We had bought a pink nylon apron for Betty. "Look at the ruffles and the fancy embroidery," she said admiringly. "I love to embroider and knit. We have two periods of needlework every week. May I show you the sweater I'm working on?" she asked. I followed her into her room. "I'm in fifth grade," she said proudly. "Here's my class schedule." As I studied the chart, I realized that the curriculum had changed very little since I had attended the *Volksschule* from 1932–36. There was the same emphasis on needlework, sewing, physical education, geography, German, and music that I remembered. "We also have nature studies and arithmetic," offered Betty. I could find no evidence of regularly scheduled history classes.

I should not have been surprised that in 1958 the curriculum of Betty's village school did not include the study of history. Perhaps the course of study had not yet been revised. In 1958 the Germans were just beginning to confront their past. Those who had lived for a dozen years under a dictatorship where all original thought and creativity was suppressed needed time to adjust to the demands of an open democratic system. The American occupation forces had made a great effort to guide the defeated population toward a new way of thinking, and that required the rewriting of the textbooks to be used in the entire school system, from kindergarten through university. The areas that had been under British control apparently required more time to accomplish this goal.

Even as I am writing this book, in 1997, the German schools are struggling to develop courses of study to teach the history of the Holocaust. Who will train the teachers? What materials and methods should be used for the different grade levels? How can the teaching of tolerance be incorporated into the curriculum?

Betty and I returned to the living room. Mr. Brotmann was showing John a newly acquired camera, Mrs. Brotmann was working in the kitchen, Annie was taking a nap, and the six-year-old was playing outside with a big red ball we had brought him. We thanked our hosts and walked back to Lüneburg.

Mr. Schmidt was standing in the doorway of the hotel. "There is an important message for you," he said. "Inspector Edel stopped by to see you. Please call him right away at his home. Let me dial for you," he said politely, and handed John the receiver.

"That's wonderful! Thank you so much!" said John with enthusiasm. He was smiling broadly. "Our court appearance has been scheduled for Thursday, October 9! Hurray!"

XXVIII

John had taped the flow chart of all the steps required for Annie's adoption on the wall above the typewriter. The first two events, Annie's physical exam and smallpox vaccination and the signing of the contract of adoption had been completed. John placed oversized red check marks on the chart to indicate our progress. "We still have a long way to go," he sighed, "and not a minute to waste!"

And so, on Monday John completed the American forms for the provision of an affidavit of support. On Tuesday we took Annie to the U.S. consulate in Hamburg so she could be seen by the U.S. Public Health Service doctor; for although Annie had been pronounced fit by the staff of the Children's Hospital in Hamburg and the Health Department in Lüneburg, it was required that an *American* physician give the final approval.

Annie was an amazingly cooperative traveler. When we found out that the station restaurant did not serve milk or sandwiches for lunch, Annie put away a large plate of oxtail soup, a hot dog, and a banana. The noise and commotion in the station's waiting room did not bother her as she napped on a makeshift "bed" between two chairs, and on the train she sat contentedly on John's lap and looked out the window. Even the bus trip back to her foster home didn't faze her.

On Wednesday we met Mrs. Brotmann and Annie at the health department clinic to have the vaccination read. Afterwards all of us went to the department store to buy brown leather boots and a pair of slippers for Annie. Then Mrs. Brotmann tied the red kerchief on the little girl's head, strapped her into the special bicycle seat, and rode off toward Neustadt.

John and I stopped at the lawyer's office to pay our first bill and to receive an official copy of the contract of adoption. "Are you ready for the big day tomorrow?" John asked me. We had never faced a judge alone before, and we doubted that the trial scenes in American movies had prepared us for our experience in a German court. We decided to visit Inspector Edel for last-minute advice and reassurance.

"Your appointment at the *Amtsgericht* (court) is at 2 P.M.," said Mr. Edel. "I thought it might be nice if the two of you, the judge, and I had the midday meal together. As Annie's legal guardian I will have to give my consent before the guardianship court can approve the contract, and I can settle this formality when I see the judge." Inspector Edel smiled. "We can relax over a good dinner and Judge Tremel can get to know you a bit. I have already made reservations at the hotel dining room."

"When does the bus for Braunsburg leave?" inquired John.

"You won't need the bus," said Inspector Edel. "I'll pick you up at your hotel at 11:30. That allows us plenty of time. Braunsburg is only about twenty-four kilometers from here.

"It just occurred to me," the inspector continued, "that you may want to spend the night in Braunsburg. I need to return to Lüneburg after dinner. The last bus leaves at 6 P.M., and the court proceedings may take longer. It would be wise to reserve space at the hotel *now*. I understand that the county fair is in full swing this week, and it might be difficult to get a room." He picked up the phone. "They know me there," he said with a twinkle in his eye.

After a brief conversation with the manager, the inspector turned to us. "If you don't mind climbing stairs, there's a room for you on the third floor."

John nodded in agreement. "That will be fine!"

When we awoke on Thursday morning we noticed that the heat had been turned on in our hotel. Fall had arrived in Lüneburg. We packed pajamas, robes, and sweaters for the overnight stay. It had turned cloudy and windy, and we were glad to be picked up by car.

Judge Tremel had arrived at the hotel before us and led us into the dining room. We noticed that he walked with a slight limp. After Inspector Edel introduced us, we shook hands and sat down at a round table that was covered with a white damask cloth. The dishes on the printed menu were more expensive than our budget allowed, but this was a special occasion. Tomorrow we would start skimping again.

I studied Judge Tremel's face. It was serious, perhaps even a bit sad. He asked us to tell him about Annie and our hopes for her future. John pulled Annie's brand new passport photo out of his wallet and passed it around. The judge examined it. "She looks intelligent," he said. "Inspector Edel has told me about her. Has she recovered from the whooping cough? Children are a great responsibility, but they also bring the greatest joy. I know," he said with a chuckle, "my wife and I have six! There is never a dull moment in our home!" The sadness had disappeared from his face.

Mr. Edel reminded us to register at the desk and to take the suitcase to our room. What a wonderful surprise to find that there was an adjoining bathroom with hot water! We freshened up and walked down. Mr. Edel was waiting for us in the lobby.

"I'll drive you to the castle," he said. Did he say "castle?" After a short distance, he stopped. "This building dates back to the Middle Ages," he explained. "It now houses the guardianship court as well as the circuit court. The drawbridge takes you across the moat to the main door."

I reached for John's hand to make sure that this wasn't a dream.

"Before I drop you off let me take you to the Elbe River, about a block away," Mr. Edel said. We got out of the car and walked to the banks of the river. "This is the border between East and West Germany," he said, pointing to the barbed-wire fence and guard towers. "Do you see that the sand has been freshly raked? If anyone should try to escape, the footprints would immediately alert the guards. Moreover, there are probably land mines hidden under the neat sand strip. Very few attempt to flee from East Germany at this spot. It is too dangerous."

This was 1958. Before us stretched the barbed wire of the twentieth century. Behind us was the moat surrounding the medieval castle. We stood in silence in the eerie, unreal reality, contemplating the barriers that separate man from man.

"We must return to the castle," the inspector reminded us. "The court is ready to hear your case."

XXIX

It was 1:50 P.M. when Inspector Edel dropped us off at the drawbridge. We hurried across the span so as not to be late for our
appointment and saw Judge Tremel standing at the massive door to
welcome us. "Let me take you to the chambers," he said. "The chairs
have been set up for you. Make yourselves comfortable. I'll be back
in just a few minutes."

John and I took stock of the surroundings: The high-ceilinged
room was probably large enough to accommodate our entire apartment back home; at the far end stood a huge desk with an ancient
lamp and a set of candlesticks, and at its right, on a metal cart, was a
round porcelain wash basin that contained a large matching pitcher.

There were some tapestries and portraits on the walls, but the light
in the room was so dim that we were unable to distinguish any
details. "Do you think they keep the place dark so as not to wake up
Sleeping Beauty?" John whispered to me. I appreciated his effort at
breaking the tension we both felt, but this was hardly the time for
jokes. The realization that the success or failure of our quest depend-
ed solely on the good will of one individual weighed heavily upon us.
We had been incredibly lucky so far, but there was no guarantee that
our good fortune would continue. In fact, according to the printed
instructions that had been handed to us by both the German and the
American authorities, we didn't stand the slightest chance of meeting
all the legal requirements governing adoptions in Germany.

A side door opened and Judge Tremel entered. We remembered the
court scenes we had seen in the movies and jumped to our feet. Slowly the judge walked to the desk (I believe he used a cane), sat down,
and looked straight at us.

"Thank you," he said. "Please sit down. The guardianship court is
now in session," he announced, and then he turned to the folders in
front of him. "I have examined all the documents and papers your

lawyer submitted and find them in good order. After our informal talk at dinner I feel confident that you, as a couple and individually, will strive to provide a warm and loving home to little Annie. According to Inspector Edel, the girl's guardian, it is in her best interest to be placed with a stable family. She has already seen too many institutions in her young life." He paused.

"It is in my discretion to waive a number of requirements in your favor," he said, and he began to read a list of statements that were couched in legalistic jargon and made little sense to me. However, I do remember two provisions, possibly because they seemed particularly absurd. The first one stated that the adoptive mother had to be at least fifty years old. The intention was to exclude the possibility of her producing natural offspring who might be favored over the adopted child, especially in matters of inheritance. The second one concerned a declaration by the adoptive parents that they were *not* entering the contract in order to acquire any assets the child might have. The intent of this clause was to protect "poor little rich girls" from being exploited, but it certainly did not apply to Annie. As far as we knew, she owned only the clothes that she was wearing on the passport photo, a light blue raincoat, and the items that we had bought for her. The rest of her belongings were the property of the orphanage. We gladly signed the formal declaration.

The judge gathered the papers together but made no effort to rise. He rested his head in his hands and appeared in deep thought. The stillness inside the castle was palpable. Outside, however, it was less peaceful. The clouds had burst, and the wind had picked up. We could hear the water rushing out of the gutters. Leaves and small twigs were pounding the narrow window panes, and then the lights began to flicker. For a fleeting moment the room was pitch dark, but then the dim lights returned.

"Don't worry," said the judge, "I have a good supply of candles in addition to the candlesticks on my desk." Soon the downpour changed into a steady rain, and the wind subsided.

Judge Tremel broke the silence. "I am glad to inform you that the guardianship court has given its official *consent* to the adoption. Thus you have completed the first step toward the issuance of the required decree of adoption. The second step consists of the *ratification* of the adoption contract before the circuit court. As you know, this final decision is usually granted only after several months. This waiting period provides a time of adjustment for the new family, and thus serves as a safeguard for all parties involved. The adoption of a child is a lifelong commitment, and the court considers each case as unique."

He looked at us earnestly. "Of course," he continued in a barely audible voice, "I will take your time constraints into consideration."

He poured a glass of water from the porcelain pitcher and took a couple of sips. "Permit me to make some personal comments," he said in a voice that betrayed deep emotion. "I must tell you that I am delighted to help you. You see, as a judge in a small town, I usually see only the negative side of the human condition, and I realize that a verdict, no matter how just, rarely serves to rehabilitate the wrongdoer."

He took a deep breath, leaned forward and continued. "The fact that you, a Jewish couple, have come from America to look for a child in the country of your birth has a special significance to me. I beg you to listen to me," he urged us. And he began to tell his story:

He was born in 1910, married in 1939, became a soldier in the German army in the same year, participated in the western campaign, and then was sent to the Russian front. In 1944, during the German retreat from the Baltic states, he was seriously wounded and lost his lower left leg.

"I was lying in a trench, barely clinging to life," he recalled. "I knew that millions of Germans, Russians, and members of the Allied forces had been killed in a senseless war brought about by the Nazis. Surely this was God's retribution for the torture and annihilation of the Jewish people. I made a vow that, if I survived, I would make it my mission to bring Christians and Jews together to foster understanding through the study of the Jewish texts. The Nazis had managed to destroy not only the Jews, but their culture, literature, drama, art, music, and science. It was a tremendous loss to what we call 'German civilization,' but gradually the works of Jewish authors have become available again in the better bookstores. We cannot undo history, but we must make every effort to prevent a repetition of the horrors of the past. We must root out those terrible diseases, ignorance and prejudice."

John nodded. "Are you feeling all right?" the judge called in an anxious voice. "You look so pale, Mr. Wolff! Have some water!"

"I am sorry to bother you with my story. You see, there really is nobody with whom I can share my heavy burden of guilt, the guilt that rests on all of us. My colleagues certainly don't want to hear of it, and my neighbors would like to forget that it was the Nazis who caused that terrible tragedy. They are too busy enjoying the amazing recovery of the German economy, in which there is virtually no unemployment. We must not permit them to forget what brought about the Holocaust!" He cleared his throat. "The problem is that most members of the young generation have never met a Jew. I belong to a Christian-Jewish study group I helped found in Hamburg, and there are communities of survivors in Hannover, Frankfurt, and Berlin. But in the small towns all traces of Jewish life have been extinguished."

The judge rose and walked haltingly toward us. "I want my children to meet a Jew in person. I want them to see that Jews are people just like us. I want them to talk to a Jew who speaks their language. I want them to ask questions. They are entitled to honest answers from a Jew, a real Jew, a human being." The judge held out his hand. "Please grant me the favor and come to my home. I want both of you to meet my wife and children." We promised to visit the Tremel family on Saturday.

The judge regained his composure, gathered the folders on his desk, and asked us to follow him across the hall to a brightly lit room. We were relieved to return to reality.

"The circuit court is now in session," announced the judge. A smile crossed his face as he added in a soft voice, "Six months have just passed! The court hereby *ratifies* the contract of adoption to which the guardianship court has previously given its *consent*." He signed several papers. "Congratulations to both of you! You are now a real family! The *decree of adoption* has now been issued and will be sent to you soon. As of this moment you assume all responsibility, financial and otherwise, for the little girl you are planning to name Rebecca Susan. Use this signed statement to complete the process of changing the child's name. You need to do that right away so that the police may issue a valid passport to Rebecca Susan Wolff. May your little Rebecca bring you much happiness!" The judge shook hands with us.

Suddenly his face turned serious again. "I am very conscious of the fact that one and a half million Jewish children were murdered in cold blood. Nothing can replace that loss. Yet, in helping you adopt Rebecca, I have made an attempt, *in a symbolic way*, to make amends for that terrible tragedy. One small child reminds us of the infinite value of each human being."

John and I were deeply moved by the judge's words. I had to struggle to keep my feelings under control as I managed to say, "Thanks for everything!"

"See you Saturday," John promised.

XXX

W
e must write to our parents tonight," said John as we walked in the drizzle to our hotel. "I wish I could see the expression on their faces when they read that they are now full-fledged grandparents!"

"Do you realize that *we* are now full-fledged *parents*?" I reminded John. "There are so many things that we need to do, quite aside from the name change, passport, quota number, visa, and boat accommodations. We need to buy a winter coat for Becky and a full wardrobe for the trip home. She weighs twenty-seven pounds, and I can't carry her around for any length of time. A stroller would come in handy, don't you agree, John?" I was thinking out loud.

"I am looking forward to putting huge, red check marks on the flow chart," mused John.

It had been an intense day. The storybook setting of the castle, the hushed atmosphere in the dim courtroom, the violent weather, and the emotional confession by the judge combined to create an unforgettable scene. This day, Thursday, October 9, 1958, marked a turning point in our lives.

Through the fog we could hear the muffled oom-pa-pa of the brass band that signaled the opening of the carnival. "Let's relax awhile in our room," said John. "Perhaps we'll have enough energy later to visit the fair. A walk to the river will do us good." He lay down and immediately fell into a deep sleep.

I felt exhausted, but my overstimulated brain kept me from sleeping. I began to compose a letter to my parents. At last I could give them definite information on our progress and congratulate them on their grandparenthood. I signed the letter "Mother Marion" and started to laugh. John stirred but did not wake up.

"Perhaps I should start working on the shopping list for Becky's things," I thought. As I wrote down the needed items, I realized that

I had no idea how much toddlers' clothes cost in Lüneburg. Would our money supply hold out? Would there be room in our suitcases for the purchases?

John sat up. "I just had the strangest nightmare," he said. "I dreamt we couldn't find our way out of the castle. Thank goodness it was only a dream! Let's go to the carnival!"

We followed a group of hotel guests down to the river's edge. As we got closer, we noticed the aroma of hot dogs and sauerkraut filling the air, and we realized how hungry we were.

The drizzle had stopped. People gathered around large metal kettles that held the steaming sauerkraut, and a line was forming at the beer-on-tap booth. There were shooting galleries and the usual wheels of fortune. A balloon man directed the crowd to a fortune teller, and an oversized fellow with red suspenders, a feather in his hat, and a cigar hanging from his mouth offered to guess anyone's age and weight. At the top of the Ferris wheel, children were dangling their legs from the swinging seats and shrieking as the giant wheel slowed down. We found a bench in a large open tent and enjoyed our supper of hot dogs, kraut, a slab of black "peasant bread," and a bottle of seltzer water. Everybody seemed to be having fun, and nobody took notice of us.

The scene could have been the midway of any county fair in America, perhaps in the Midwest, had it not been for the dark silence and the freshly raked earth on the opposite river bank. The drinking crowd seemed oblivious of the barbed wire and the guard tower. Oom-pa-pa, oom-pa-pa played the band. This was Germany in 1958.

The next day, Friday, October 10, we took the early morning bus to Lüneburg. The air was crisp and dry; the streets were uncrowded, since most stores had not yet opened; pedestrians in heavy jackets were hurrying to their office jobs. We stopped at the bakery to buy freshly baked honey buns and returned to our hotel.

"It's eight o'clock," said John pointing to the bugle sticking out of the window of the church tower. "Listen to the wake up call! It really makes me feel at home," he said.

John took the red marker out of the desk drawer. He began checking off on the flow chart our latest accomplishments. "Five check marks down," he counted, "only six more to go! If our luck continues, we have a pretty good chance to meet the deadline," he said. "It all depends on the American consulates," I added.

After breakfast John visited Inspector Edel at the *Jugendamt* to tell him the good news and to thank him for his help. The petition to change Annie's name to Rebecca Susan Wolff had been approved.

"I will help you with the other formalities," Inspector Edel assured John. "Tomorrow we need to go to the city hall where a new birth certificate will be issued. Your name and your wife's name will then appear as those of Rebecca's parents. This document is extremely important because it provides the information for Rebecca's passport. Without the passport you will not be able to obtain a visa. You do have the required photos, don't you?" Mr. Edel asked.

"Oh yes," replied John, and he handed him an envelope containing two passport pictures. "We have already sent copies to Rebecca's new grandparents in America."

We walked to the municipal telephone building to make two important long-distance calls. The first one was to Mr. Fisher, our friend at the American consulate in Frankfurt. He was delighted to hear of our success and advised us to submit our petition for a "preference quota number" to the Frankfurt consulate.

"Little Rebecca will immigrate under the German quota. As the child of American citizens, however, she will be given preference. I suppose you have already completed the required forms. Be sure you ask for me when you arrive at the consulate on Monday," he advised us.

The second call was to my uncle Erwin Lichtenstein, who had been so supportive in the early days of our search. We asked him to reserve a room for us at Pension Feldberg for Monday night, since the trip from Lüneburg to Frankfurt took eight hours and we needed to stay overnight before returning the next day. If we were successful in having the quota petition approved there would be no need for another trip to Frankfurt. It would be wonderful to have a last family reunion before our return to America.

On Saturday morning we visited Becky at the Brotmanns'. We explained to Becky's foster parents that the little girl was now legally ours and that the *Jugendamt* was no longer responsible for her. John and Mr. Brotmann agreed on the amount we would owe for Becky's care from October 10 through October 26. We would pay in two installments. Of course, we would come and visit as often as possible so that Becky would become used to us and her new name.

As we walked back to Lüneburg we discussed the state of our financial reserves. Large expenses loomed ahead of us. John reassured me that he had budgeted for them. In case of an emergency, he could wire our bank at home and have funds transferred to our Lüneburg account.

"It wouldn't hurt to cut down on the fancy meals," he said. Just then I spotted a sign in the window of an apartment building. *Mittagstisch*, it proclaimed. A *Mittagstisch* is a dining room in a private home that features homecooked meals. Often the operation is run by a widow who needs the additional income to supplement a meager pension. The food is usually very simple, inexpensive, but nourishing. Perhaps eating at a *Mittagstisch* would help cut our expenses, we thought.

We climbed the stairs, followed the cooking odor, and walked through a door that had been left ajar. Three or four tables had been set; two people were seated at a corner table. An elderly woman came out of the kitchen to greet us.

"What are you serving today?" John inquired.

"I don't have a menu," said the woman. "Today I have prepared raisin soup, hard-boiled eggs, and boiled potatoes."

John looked dubious, but I felt it would be impolite to leave, so we ordered. The hot soup consisted of a white sauce with a handful of raisins thrown in. It was very sweet and a bit salty at the same time. When we had finished, the woman came to remove the dishes. She put a bowl of boiled potatoes on the table and placed two hard-boiled eggs on each plate. We asked for a cup of tea.

"I wish I had vitamin pills," remarked John. The meal was ridiculously cheap, but on the way home we stopped to buy fresh tomatoes, apples, and strawberry yogurt and used up all the money we had saved.

John remembered his appointment with Inspector Edel at the city hall to obtain the amended birth certificate for Rebecca. Since my presence was not required, I stopped at Lüneburg's largest bookstore and managed to find a volume on the history of the United States and a paperback entitled *History of the Jews*. When I got back to the hotel, I leafed through them. There were many colorful pictures in both books and a number of fold-out maps. They were written in German, of course, and each had an index for easy reference. "To the Tremel family with best wishes," I wrote in each book above our signatures.

John returned. He looked triumphant. "Here's the new official birth certificate and six photocopies, all notarized, of course. You can never have too many documents," he chuckled. "Two more red check marks down on the flow chart and four more to go!"

"Promise me you won't be angry," I begged John. "I have developed a splitting headache, a sick migraine, and I feel vile. Could you possibly visit Judge Tremel and his family without me? I can't figure out what brought this on. Do you think it was the raisin soup?" I asked.

"You do look green," John confirmed, "but I think it's the excitement of the last couple of days that is getting to you. Try to get some sleep. You need to relax. Okay, I'll go by myself but I won't stay long," John said.

It was dark when John returned. "I had a nice visit," he said. "Mrs. Tremel had baked an apple strudel, and the children were very friendly. They were very interested in the fact that I had come from the 'New World.' I think they were disappointed that I wasn't dressed like an Indian chief. I gave each one an American coin, an Indianhead nickel, as consolation. Judge Tremel explained to the children that I was Jewish, but they didn't seem impressed. Obviously they saw nothing remarkable in me, neither in my appearance nor in my demeanor. They asked me about the Grand Canyon. Was it true that everyone had to own a car to get around? Is there still a 'Wild West' where people shoot each other?"

If Judge Tremel's aim was to prove to his children that Jews were just like the rest of humanity, he had certainly succeeded. "It was an easy assignment," said John modestly, "but I wish you could have been well enough to come along."

On Sunday my energy had returned. We spent the morning sorting our clothes into "needed" and "not needed" piles. Since mid-October in Lüneburg is like mid-December in Washington, the time for summer garments had passed. By shipping the unnecessary clothes back to America we would create room in our suitcases for Becky's things. The forecast for next week called for rain and strong winds. We packed sweaters, umbrellas, and raincoats for our trip to Frankfurt and then went downstairs to have a bowl of oxtail soup in the hotel restaurant. In the evening we attended another organ recital at St. John's Church. It was a good way to mark the end of our eighth week in Europe. And what a week it had been!

XXXI

On Monday we left at the crack of dawn to catch the 7:30 train to Hannover, where we had to transfer to the Frankfurt Express. Since we had traveled this way many times before, the lovely landscape had lost its charm and the eight-hour trip seemed interminable. We caught a taxi from the station to the American consulate and arrived shortly before closing time. Mr. Fisher was awaiting us. He smiled at us encouragingly and referred us to his secretary. We presented the petition for a preference quota number and a notarized copy of the decree of adoption and, in an amazing display of efficiency, the petition was granted within half an hour. No doubt Mr. Fisher had helped matters along. We thanked him for his support and guidance throughout our search.

It had begun to rain. The offices were letting out, and soon the rush hour and resulting traffic jams took on American proportions. Again we were lucky to spot a taxicab to take us to Pension Feldberg, where we were to meet my relatives, the Lichtensteins. Uncle Erwin, Aunt Lotte, Cousin Ruth, and her younger sister, Hannah, were eagerly waiting for us. I had not seen Hannah since 1939, when both of us were fourteen. And now she had flown in from Israel to spend a few days with us and her family. As we sat around the table at Erwin's favorite restaurant, we reported on the happy end to our search. When Hannah passed around photos of her three children, we showed the picture of *our* new daughter. It was the fourth day of our parenthood, and Erwin used the opportunity to propose a toast to the expanding family circle.

There was so much to celebrate! Only four weeks earlier we had left Frankfurt without a clue to what the future might hold. Yet with the help of four extraordinary people and a series of unexplained coincidences, the puzzle pieces had fallen into place. Our good fortune had begun with Mr. Schneider, the social worker in Giessen.

"I remember the sealed letter he gave you and the box of chocolates he sent you," said Erwin.

"Who were the other three?" asked Aunt Lotte.

As we tried to describe the help Inspector Edel, Ilse Heins, and Judge Tremel had given us, we realized that the story sounded almost too fantastic to be true. "Some day you should write a book," said Erwin.

The next morning the six of us had breakfast in the pension. "Let's not wait another nineteen years for the next reunion," said Ruth.

"You must come and visit us in Israel," added Hannah, "with Becky, of course." We promised.

We left the pension in pouring rain. Before heading for the train station we stopped at a candy store. We selected a two-pound box of assorted chocolates and had it gift-wrapped for mailing. "Dear Mr. Schneider," we wrote on the accompanying card, "the adoption went through. We are now the parents of twenty-one-months-old Rebecca. Thanks for everything!"

After a dreary and boring train ride, we arrived in Lüneburg at 8 P.M., had supper at the station, and walked to our hotel. The umbrella came in handy. John put another red check mark on the flow chart. "Do you realize that we spent over sixteen hours on the train for a transaction that took thirty minutes?" he asked. "Meeting with the Lichtensteins one more time made it worthwhile," I replied.

On Wednesday morning John visited the *Jugendamt* to pick up Becky's passport. He then phoned the American consulate in Hamburg to arrange for the visa.

"I've got the quota number for Becky, and the passport, so getting the visa should present no problem," he said to me as we had a quick lunch together. I'll be back for dinner. You can use the time to buy clothes for Becky."

I walked to the town's biggest department store and took the elevator to the children's department. Several salesladies converged on me, the only customer on the floor. They helped me select two pairs of pajamas, two cotton baby blankets, six undershirts, six underpants, four long-sleeved polo shirts, two corduroy overalls, knee-high socks, a brush, and a comb. The most important item, a heavy winter coat, took longer to choose. Mrs. Brotmann had given me Becky's measurements to be sure. "You can't always trust the size on the label," she had warned me. At last I picked a bright red plush coat that had a pointed hood with drawstrings and soft flannel lining.

"Your little girl will look adorable in this coat. Everyone will call her Little Red Riding Hood," said the saleslady with a broad smile. She packed the purchases into two shopping bags with handles. Loaded down with the bulky packages, I hurried through the rain and was glad when I reached our cozy room. I took off my soaked shoes and stockings, drank a cup of tea, and crawled into bed.

John returned later than I had expected. "Did you get the visa?" I asked anxiously.

"Oh yes," John said. "I also stopped at a bookstore and a wonderful music store," he confessed. "I needed a new bow for my violin, and I found exactly what I wanted."

"You look so tired," I said. "Let's go downstairs and have a bite to eat."

"I am not hungry," John protested. "I just feel utterly exhausted. Thank goodness we don't need to travel tomorrow. Do you realize that we have almost completed the items on the flow chart? All we still need is the ticket for Becky's passage on the *Gripsholm*." He shivered, staggered to the sink, and vomited. I fixed him a cup of tea and tucked him into bed.

I added two more red check marks on the flow chart. "Only one more to go," I said. "You've done a terrific job!" John didn't hear me; he was already fast asleep.

XXXII

At this point in our story, I must once again interrupt the narrative briefly in order to provide historical background material for this chapter.

From the day Hitler came to power (January 30, 1933), the persecution of the Jews was carried on systematically and with ever-increasing intensity. During the first phase the "War Against the Jews" was fought silently through legislation aimed at depriving Jewish citizens of their professions, their livelihood, their dignity, their civil rights, their education, and their citizenship. About one third of Germany's Jewish population of 500,000 escaped before 1938. The second phase, culminating in the burning of the synagogues and the deportation of 30,000 men and boys to the concentration camps of Dachau, Buchenwald, and Sachsenhausen on November 9 through 10, 1938, brought the "War Against the Jews" into the open for all to see. On January 30, 1939, Hitler boasted to the world that he would solve the Jewish problem by the total destruction of the Jewish race in Europe. There was no reason to doubt his word; yet the world ignored him. Between November 1938 and the outbreak of World War II on September 3, 1939, another third of German Jews managed to flee to any country that would admit them.

Many more lives could have been saved had the United States relaxed its quota system and had Great Britain admitted refugees, especially children, into Palestine. After the outbreak of the war, and for part of 1940, several thousand Jews miraculously succeeded in escaping, my immediate family among them. We all know what happened to those Jews who were trapped in Germany: thousands chose death by their own hands; some died of natural causes; some went into hiding; some survived the camps. The rest were exterminated.

After November 1938, Holland, Belgium, and France opened their doors to Jewish children. Great Britain, while denying entry to

Palestine to 10,000 children, at last allowed 10,000 unaccompanied youngsters to find a "temporary" haven in England. Desperate Jewish parents made the painful decision to send their children away in an effort to save their young lives. The separation, they told their children, would be temporary and soon the families would be reunited. The majority of the members of the *Kindertransport* (Children's Transports), however, waited in vain; they would discover after the war that they were the only survivors. Their parents and younger siblings were among the six million who perished in the Holocaust.

Throughout the spring and summer of 1939, children with identification tags on strings dangling from their necks, and knapsacks on their backs would crowd the platforms of the train stations and hang out of the windows of the packed *Kindertransport* trains that would take them to their sponsors in England and Scotland.

Among those who waved goodbye to their parents on June 5, 1939, were John Wolff and his sister Marianne. John had just turned fourteen, and Marianne would be eleven in July. Their destination was Scarborough on the Yorkshire coast where for the next five and a half years they were to live in the home of the Dobson family. John and Marianne could not have wished for a more loving, secure home. When they came to the United States in January 1945 to rejoin their parents (who had been saved by Swedish friends shortly before the war broke out), they left part of their hearts in England with the generous Dobson family.

Let's resume our story: On October 15, 1958, we had completed all the formalities concerning Becky's adoption and immigration and still had about a week to spare before our return to the United States. It was the perfect opportunity to visit the Dobsons and to renew the ties with the family to whom John owed his life.

After a restful night, John was much better. He felt energized by the thought that after a dozen years he would see Ma Dobson and his three foster siblings again. (Pa Dobson, who had been a role model to the adolescent John, had died in the interim). After a hearty breakfast we walked to the telephone building to place calls to London and Scarborough.

I could hear the excitement in John's voice. "We'll be in London on Saturday the eighteenth, spend a week traveling, and return on the twenty-fifth via the Harwich-Hook of Holland boat to the continent," he told Margaret, his foster sister. "I hope I can arrange to meet all of my relatives and friends during that short time," he added.

We went to the travel bureau, stuffed our briefcase with train schedules, maps, and colorful brochures, bought train and ferry tickets, and exchanged dollars for British currency and international traveler's cheques. Mindful of the channel's rough waters in late October, we stopped at an apothecary shop for seasickness pills, headache tablets, and facial tissues.

"I need to call Inspector Edel and inform him of our plans," said John. "Becky can stay with the Brotmanns. We expect to return to Lüneburg on Sunday, October 26, and leave on Monday morning *with* Becky for Bremen. The *Gripsholm* will leave Bremerhaven on Wednesday afternoon. There are still many details to be worked out," he sighed.

"I hope we aren't overdoing the nomadic life," I said. "Horrors, we'll miss bath night on Friday!"

"I'll have to brush up on my Yorkshire dialect," John joked as we began to pack our suitcases. "We definitely need the raincoats, the umbrellas, and heavy sweaters. It gets very cold in Scarborough, you know," he reminded me, "but Ma always has hot water bottles to warm up the clammy sheets."

It was my first trip to England and the thought of thick fog and ineffective fireplaces did not appeal to me.

"Let's not worry about the climate," said John. "Let's concentrate on planning our itinerary." And he spread out the map on the table.

Before we left Lüneburg on Friday, we stopped at the lawyer's office to have all our documents photocopied and notarized. Dr. König offered to keep our papers in his office safe until our return. Miss Long promised to bring the entire file to the hotel early on Monday, the 27th of October, the day we were to leave Lüneburg with Becky.

We had lunch at the railroad station, took the local train to Hamburg, and transferred to the Skandinavia-London Express. We traveled west through Holland, via Rotterdam to the Hook of Holland. It was midnight when we boarded the *Amsterdam*, the cross-channel ferry-boat. Men and women were assigned to separate quarters. Each cabin consisted of four berths, two upper and two lower. I was given an upper berth and began a conversation with my cabinmates, a friendly group. As the boat left the harbor we stretched out, eager to get some sleep. Soon the boat began to roll in the choppy seas. All of my companions became violently seasick. I was lucky and managed to keep my dinner down, perhaps thanks to the seasickness pills, but it was impossible to sleep amid the stench and the loud moaning of the ill passengers. About 6:30 A.M. we were aroused by a knock on the door. A stewardess urged us to get dressed and assemble on deck for breakfast. I gathered my things together, tottered upstairs, and was relieved to find John, who was already looking for me. He had been dreadfully sick, and he looked pale and drawn. We found seats at a table with a young family. They were talking loud and fast and seemed quite agitated. I could not understand a word they were saying.

"What language are they speaking?" I whispered to John.

"It's English," he laughed. "Well, actually, it's Cockney. You'll understand it once you get used to it," he consoled me.

A steward handed out crackers and offered a choice of tea or coffee. I opted for what he said was coffee. It was my first mistake: When in England always order tea! I had a lot to learn.

There was no time to linger. We were glad to get off the boat and onto the 8:15 train to London, where Margaret was going to meet us.

John had drawn up a detailed itinerary and, thanks to the efficient British Railways, we were able to stick to our schedule. Saturday and Sunday we stayed with Margaret, John's foster sister. She had married a well-known journalist.

There were three lively children between six and eleven years old, all of them eager to show us nearby Kenwood Park. "It rains all the time here," explained nine-year-old Rachel, "so it's quite all right to step on the grass!"

In the evening we sat around the fire talking about the early days and the war years when John had lived with the Dobsons. "Do you remember?" and "whatever happened to so-and-so?" Margaret and John asked again and again, attempting to catch up with the happenings of thirteen years. Then we passed around the photograph of little Becky and the talk turned to the future.

The next morning we left for Nottingham to visit John's foster brothers, Ken, a high school teacher, and Frank, the youngest of the foster siblings. Ken and his wife, Jean, and their three children lived in a suburb of Nottingham. In their amazing self-confidence and self-sufficiency they reminded me of what I imagined American homesteaders to have been. In 1958 they had no car and no telephone. Next to their home Ken had built a greenhouse so that vine-ripened tomatoes were available all year 'round. There was a large plot of land where all kinds of vegetables were grown, even potatoes and celery. In his spare time Ken was an avid cabinetmaker and justly proud of the pieces of furniture he built.

In the evening we met friends and neighbors of Ken and Jean. The conversation was lively and informative as we exchanged ideas on politics, education, and adoption laws. Again I realized how fortunate John and his sister had been to be rescued by such intelligent and loving people.

On Wednesday we continued our trip to Manchester to visit two of John's cousins, siblings of the young girl who had died at Bergen-Belsen. It was a bittersweet reunion. While we were happy to be together, we could not help thinking of those we had lost. The boys, David and Peter, however, were proud first-generation Englishmen. They took us on a walk through the neighborhood and enthusiastically told us about their schools and soccer games.

The next morning we left for Scarborough, Yorkshire, John's hometown for most of his teenage years.

"Let me tell you about the town," John said. "During peacetime it was a seaside resort on the North Sea. The coast is quite steep there, and a winding path led through a park down to the beach. Ma and Pa Dobson owned a hotel on the oceanfront, and their three children and the two little refugees pitched in to help with the never-ending chores. When we arrived in Scarborough in June 1939, the summer season was just beginning. I remember the dining room crowded with vacationing families, the stacks of dishes, and the piles of bed linens. I used to help Ma Dobson stretch and fold the freshly laundered sheets."

The war, of course, changed all that. Instead of tourists, British military officers were billeted in the hotel. During the "Blitz,"

German bombers that attacked industrial cities in northern England would occasionally empty their remaining deadly cargo on Scarborough.

"I remember one night when we huddled under the massive dining table, as we heard the bombs fall. The next morning we realized that the house three doors down had been hit. Only a large crater remained."

There was little to eat and not enough coal to heat the homes in those dark days. "People stuck together and did what needed to be done. I can't remember anyone complaining," recalled John. "The British are stoic on the outside but very warm on the inside. We knew that it was a fight for Britain's survival."

After the death of Pa Dobson, the hotel was sold and Ma moved to a little brick townhouse, where she was living alone when we came to visit.

"Oh, John," she said, hugging him. "When you were stationed in Germany with the American forces, you came to see me. I think it was in 1946, and I remember that you had already acquired that awful American twang. I hope you haven't forgotten the real English," she said in her heavy Yorkshire dialect. "You are just in time for high tea. Let me put the kettle on the fire, while you go upstairs. The bottles are on your bed; you'll need them tonight."

We climbed the stairs to the guest room. "I remember the bedspreads," John said, "and the smell of the disinfectant soap. I feel I've come home!"

Ma was waiting for us at the table. "It's so good to have both of you here! John was just a boy when he came to us, and now he's a married man and a new father. It's hard to keep up with the times. Let me get the kettle," she said as she went into the kitchen. "Oh dear," we heard her say breathlessly, "would you believe I forgot to turn on the gas! This has *never* happened before! It must be all the excitement about seeing you again! How embarrassing!" We all laughed.

Ma told us about her six grandchildren; John showed pictures of "little Marianne," his sister; and then the talk turned to Becky. "You must be tired," said Ma. "We can talk more tomorrow."

The next day, Friday, we visited Scarborough Boys High School, where John had graduated in 1943. Not every English child had the privilege of going to high school beyond the compulsory attendance age of fourteen, but John and his sister were especially fortunate in having come to Scarborough and the Dobsons. The generous townspeople had taken up a collection to pay the tuition for the young refugees in order to enable both of them to graduate!

We knocked on the door of the principal's office, and Mr. Marsden himself came to the door. "Hans!" he exclaimed in complete surprise. "Our old boy has returned. Let me take you to your former teachers," he said as he led us from classroom to classroom.

What followed next was an unbelievable scene: no matter what subject or what lesson was being taught, the teachers rushed to the door, embraced John, and interrupted the classes to tell the boys about the "old boy who had come back." John looked embarrassed by all the praise that was being heaped upon him. He is not the kind who enjoys being in the limelight, but he held up remarkably well.

Mr. Marsden had come along into the first classroom. "Boys," he said to a group of fifteen-year-olds, "this is Dr. Wolff. He came to us from Germany as a Jewish refugee, and during the war he was classified as an 'enemy alien.' In 1943 he graduated from this school with the highest average in his class. You will find his name on the plaque in the assembly hall with those of the boys who were awarded university scholarships. Hans Wolff represents the class of 1943."

He stopped for a moment, then continued. "You have to remember that 1943 was in the midst of the war against Hitler. I am sure you have heard recordings of Churchill's speeches. And here a full scholarship was awarded to this 'enemy alien,' this Jewish boy who had come to live with a family in Scarborough! I have never been more proud of our country and the British tradition of fair play than I was on that day," he proclaimed in a quivering voice. The boys sat in silence.

"Unfortunately, I could not make use of the scholarship," explained John. "Because of the war I opted to serve on the land. But I will always be grateful for the honor. It's also nice to see one's name in gold," he added with a smile. "But nobody calls me Hans any more. When I joined the United States Army, I became *John*!"

Mr. Marsden returned to his office, and John and I continued the rounds on our own. At mid-morning break we were invited into the teachers' lounge for a cup of cocoa, many handshakes, and good-natured backslapping. Then the teachers returned to their classes, and we went back to Ma Dobson.

The next morning Ma came along to the station. "Remember to change trains in York," she said. She reached for John's hand. "When you left in 1946, I thought I would never see you again," she said softly, "and now you have come back. But I am sure that this will be the last time I see you. I am getting old."

The train was pulling in. I gave Ma a quick, tight hug. "We'll prove you wrong," I called. "We promise to come back!" And then we boarded the train. Ma Dobson stood on the platform and waved. (In 1965 we *did* return to England to introduce Becky to Ma Dobson.)

Margaret and her husband met us at the station when we arrived in London. We stopped briefly at their house and reported on the week's events. My experiences in England convinced me that the stories I had heard about the cold, unemotional English were utterly false. I will not forget the unfailing courtesy of the train passengers, the civility of the officials, and the quiet good humor of the people who waited patiently in long queues at the bus stops. While I criticize the refugee policies of the British government in the thirties and forties, I have nothing but admiration and deep affection for the British people themselves.

XXXIII

Late Saturday night we boarded the channel boat for Holland. After a smooth crossing, we arrived on the continent at 6 A.M. and were greeted by a traditional Dutch breakfast of rolls, butter, soft-boiled eggs, and cups of fragrant, steaming java with cream. The intoxicating aroma brought back memories of my stay in Rotterdam in November 1939. Only a few months later, the old city was totally destroyed by German bombs, and 30,000 civilians were killed. In 1958, however, there were no traces of destruction. From our train window we could see a modern city whose sleek glass buildings glistened in the morning sunshine.

When we returned to our hotel in Lüneburg in the late afternoon, a pile of mail was waiting for us. We were glad to see a letter from the Swedish-American Line. "We are sorry to inform you that we are unable to change your original reservations," the letter said. "We will, however, place a crib in the two-berth stateroom to accommodate one child under two years of age."

"Don't worry," said John, "it's only for eight nights. We'll manage somehow!"

"Look John," I said, "there is a handwritten letter from Mr. Schneider in Giessen. You *must* read it!" I shoved the paper under John's nose.

Mr. Schneider had written this letter in reply to one in which we had informed him that we had completed the legal adoption procedures and that the three of us were about to leave for the United States. We had also thanked him for his personal interest in our cause and his steady support which made our success possible. Here is John's verbatim translation:

Giessen, October 17, 1958
Dear Wolff Family,

I was grateful to hear that you can now be a complete family. I wish you and your child the best of luck, joy, and contentment.

I sincerely thank you for your words of appreciation and good will, and I want to assure you again that it was a pleasure for me to be of assistance. I did it not only in the awareness that in this way I could make it possible for one child to find happy and affectionate parents, but also out of the feeling that we owe a great debt of gratitude to our [Jewish] sisters and brothers and that there is a lot for which we need to make amends.

For all your kindness my heartfelt thanks.
Sincerely,
Schneider

John read the letter slowly. He looked at me. "This explains a lot," he said. "Somehow I always suspected that Mr. Schneider had gone out of his way to help us. Remember, he was the one who really started the ball rolling," he said, nodding his head. "The box of chocolates was only a sweet gesture; it was the magic of that sealed letter that was the decisive factor in our search. I suppose we'll never find out what message the envelope contained, but it certainly had a mysterious power over those who read it," John said.

"I always felt that Mr. Schneider was a very special person," I added. "I am only sorry that we didn't have time to get to know him better."

We decided to have dinner in the hotel. "This is our last night in Lüneburg," remarked John, "and also the end of our tenth week in Europe. Every item on the flow chart has been checked off! Unbelievable! Let's splurge on our last dinner here," he said to my surprise. "This occasion definitely calls for *Wiener Schnitzel*!" (veal cutlet).

Mr. Schmidt stopped at our table. "There is a phone call for you," he said. John got up to take the call. "It was Miss Heins," he said as he returned. "She said that she missed us yesterday when she came to the hotel to say goodbye."

"Perhaps that was a blessing in disguise," I said. "You know how I hate goodbyes. I think it has something to do with my past."

"I wish we could take Miss Heins along with us to America," John added.

"I want to settle our hotel bill tonight," John continued. "There will be too much excitement tomorrow morning. Remember, we must be at the train station at ten with all our luggage *and* with Becky. Please go upstairs and start packing. Let's leave the pots and dishes here as our legacy to Mr. Schmidt," he joked.

In our nomadic life we had become experts at stuffing suitcases of different sizes for various occasions. Our last packing job in Europe, however, proved to be the most challenging. There were now three people to pack for and, since we needed to spend two more nights in a hotel before boarding the *Gripsholm*, we needed to separate the overnight items from the clothes we would wear on the ocean liner. By shipping the summer garments to America a few weeks earlier, we had created room in the two large suitcases.

I was sorting out our belongings when John joined me to make the inevitable lists. We filled the two large cases, one overnighter, and one backpack with Becky's essentials, toys, the immersion heater, and the can opener. The leather briefcase still had room for the vital documents that were kept in the lawyer's safe.

We set the alarm for 7 A.M. and crawled into bed. As usual, John was asleep the minute his head hit the pillow, while I tossed and turned, fighting an anxiety attack concerning missing documents, lost luggage, a stolen handbag, and becoming separated from John or Becky. Moreover, I couldn't help thinking about Mrs. Brotmann's giving up Becky. She had nursed the little girl through the whooping cough and cared for her for seven weeks. I had seen how attached she had become to her foster child, and I could imagine how difficult it would be to part with her. And how would Becky react? At last fatigue won out, and I fell asleep.

We awoke before the alarm went off. John dressed quickly and hurried to the bakery across the street to buy fresh breakfast pastries while I fixed hot chocolate and opened a can of orange juice for our "last" breakfast. In addition to the pots and dishes, Mr. Schmidt was to inherit the wooden crate with the leftover mustard, salt shaker, pot holders, dry spaghetti, an unopened can of condensed milk, and half a jar of instant coffee.

We finished packing, checked the closets, the bureau drawers, and the window sill, looked under the beds, and began to move our luggage, one piece at a time, down the stairs to the dining room. Then we stepped outside to take a long last look at the houses on Am Sande and St. John's Church. Just then the bugler sounded the familiar 8 A.M. wake-up call. "I'll miss that guy," muttered John.

Miss Long, the lawyer's secretary, arrived a few minutes later. She brought us the large manila envelope containing our documents and the notarized photocopies. John spread the pages out on the banquet table, and Miss Long checked them off her list. "We thank you for your excellent work," said John. "I am so glad things worked out for you," responded Miss Long. "Dr. König also sends you his best regards."

John slipped the envelope into his briefcase. Carefully he buried the case on the bottom of the overnighter. "You must *never* take your eyes off this suitcase," he reminded me solemnly. "Our future depends on it! Remember, you have your passport in your purse. I carry Becky's passport and mine in the special travel wallet in the inside pocket of my jacket."

Miss Mann, the social worker who had accompanied John and Becky to the Children's Hospital in Hamburg, appeared with Becky. "Here is your new daughter," she said, handing me the child. "Congratulations to all of you!"

"I hope Mrs. Brotmann wasn't too upset," I whispered to Miss Mann.

"It's part of being a foster mother," replied the social worker calmly. "If you had not adopted the child, she would have returned to Miss Heins's orphanage anyway. Next week I'll take a newborn to Mrs. Brotmann. She knows that all placements are temporary." She paused. "Inspector Edel told me that he would come and drive you all to the station. He should be here very soon." She left quietly.

We sat around a small table and entertained Becky. She was fascinated with a set of plastic farm animals we had bought. "Say 'piggy,'" coaxed John. "Piggy," repeated Becky.

"She's already speaking English!" laughed John.

"Say 'Mommy,'" I said, hugging her. "You are my best girl!"

Mr. Edel stopped his car in front of the hotel. "I thought you might need help with the luggage," he said. "Mother can carry Becky. Let's put the cases in the trunk." John held on to the overnighter. He sat in front next to Mr. Edel while Becky and I and the backpack occupied the back seat. Mr. Schmidt stood at the door and waved to us. We arrived at the railroad station in plenty of time for the 10:15 train to Bremen. Mr. Edel unloaded the car, accompanied us to the platform, and waited with us for the train.

"We don't know how to thank you for your kindness," said John. "Give our best regards to your wife!" The inspector helped us board the coach. "Goodbye, Lüneburg," we waved as the train pulled out.

XXXIV

The two-hour trip to Bremen provided a brief respite from our busy schedule. Becky sat on John's lap and gazed out the window. When she tired, he cradled her in his arms. "You are *our* Becky now," he whispered, as if needing to reassure himself. For ten weeks we had struggled to reach this state of parenthood. The documents in the briefcase *proved* that we were the parents of our chosen little girl, but our emotions had not yet caught up with the reality. We were hoping that the coming days would help us bond as a family, three people who were completely dependent on each other, who had chosen to love and trust each other. We felt confident that if we only heeded our instincts we could overcome any obstacles that might arise.

The train approached Bremen. We bundled Becky in her new red plush coat, gathered our hand luggage, and moved toward the front of the coach where the two suitcases were stored. "Let me help you," said a young man. "I see you have your hands full with the little girl." We gladly accepted his offer.

A taxi took us to a modern hotel where we had reserved a room for three. Bellhops in red uniforms were waiting to help us get installed. *"Essen!"* (let's eat!) said Becky. We used our very own private bathroom. *"Allein machen,"* (I can do it without help) Becky assured us, and then we walked down the wide, carpeted stairs to the restaurant.

We could see by the menu that the hotel catered to businessmen rather than young families; there was a large selection of beers and wines, but milk was unobtainable. We ordered the old standby, oxtail soup, and shared meatloaf, cabbage, and mashed potatoes with Becky. John suggested a raspberry fruit drink as a beverage. We persuaded the waiter to let Becky sit on a telephone book, since booster chairs were not available. A number of patrons in coats and ties stared at us critically. An elderly man passed our table and said loudly, "What a bother to drag babies around hotels!"

"It's a pleasure!" I replied emphatically. The man shrugged his shoulders and kept on walking.

"You must learn to ignore stupid remarks. This is Rule Number One for all parents, but especially for adoptive parents," John explained. "Not every comment or question deserves an answer." How right he was! Where had he acquired such wisdom?

We returned to our room. "Look, Becky," I said pulling her favorite plastic doll out of the backpack. "Püppi!" squealed Becky, overjoyed. We bedded *both* of them down for a nap. *"Hei-a, hei-a,"* (nighty-night) I said, and soon John and I followed their example.

When we awoke in mid-afternoon we felt refreshed and ready to explore the neighborhood. *"Pielen,"* (*spielen*, play) demanded Becky. Luckily, we found a small park nearby. It had benches on pebbled paths. Becky picked up a handful of stones, sat down, and poured gravel from one hand into the other. We observed in silence.

"I bet she misses the yard and her plum tree," I remarked. "Let's look for a fruit stand. I wouldn't mind some plums or an apple myself." I helped Becky put the stones down, picked her up and gently beat the dust off her overalls.

"Let's go," said John. We discovered a small store that not only sold fruit but made sandwiches to order. "That solves our problem," I said. "We can have a picnic in our hotel room."

"A bath for Becky would not be a luxury," I joked, noting that her hair and face were covered with fine dust. I filled the tub with about eight inches of water and eased Becky into it. Plastic Püppi floated on the water, and Becky proceeded to wash the doll. *"Haare sauber,"* (hair clean) she said and began rubbing soap suds into her own hair. I turned on the shower very gently to rinse Becky's hair.

"Now it's time to come out! Look, Mommy has a big towel," I coaxed.

"Nein!" (no) she said defiantly.

"John, come here," I called. "Do you remember Mrs. Brotmann telling us that this child hates water? Look at her! We have a fish! She'll be a great swimmer!"

"You get her out," replied John. I remembered Becky's passion for plums. *"Pflaumen,"* I said holding a plum in my hand. She agreed to come out. I wrapped her in the huge bath towel and rubbed her dry.

Her hair was soft and shiny, and her little face was radiant. I found her pajamas in the backpack, as well as a comb and toothbrush. We had our sandwiches, fruit, and soda water. Soon Becky and Püppi were asleep in the big bed, John was writing letters to his parents and his foster family in England, and I was having a "bath day" on Monday, October 27.

The next morning we had pancakes with applesauce for breakfast. John reminded me that the two large suitcases were to be checked in at the shipping company that morning. They would be trucked to Bremerhaven and loaded on the *Gripsholm* on Wednesday morning, long before any passengers were allowed to board.

"I'll take a cab and should be back before lunch," he assured me. Becky and I returned to our room and spent the morning playing with the farm animals and getting to know each other. When John returned at noontime, he was relieved that our luggage had been reduced to the overnighter and the backpack.

Bremen, a city of half a million people, has all kinds of specialty stores. We had no problem finding a sturdy collapsible stroller for Becky. Its large storage net served as a useful shopping bag. Becky immediately climbed into the stroller and loved being taken on long walks. We also bought a leather harness, a device that proved to be a lifesaver for our lively toddler.

On Wednesday morning we took the train to Bremerhaven, the port where John and I had arrived on the *Kungsholm* on Sunday, August 17. And now there were three of us lining up for the customs inspection, the passport check, the reservations check, and the luggage identification. Becky's stroller was decorated with stickers and tags saying "Swedish-American Line," and so were the overnight bag and backpack.

The passengers were kept waiting for an hour and a half before they were allowed to board the *Gripsholm*, which was anchored at the end of the dock.

"You and Becky wait for me right here," said John, leaving me with the overnighter, backpack, and Becky in her harness in the stroller. He was headed for the currency exchange office. Time passed. Becky and I began to munch on fruit and cookies. I kept my eyes glued on the overnighter.

"All passengers will embark! Have your passes ready!" blared the loudspeaker. I watched the people as they balanced themselves precariously on the steep gangplank, wondering how I could possibly manage with the bags, stroller, and Becky.

A woman in a Red Cross uniform approached me. "Are you a passenger on the *Gripsholm*?" she yelled above the din. I nodded my head. "Where is the father of this child?" she asked.

"He's exchanging some money," I offered. "I wish he'd come soon."

"Let me take the child," the woman said. "Put your bags on the stroller and follow me to the gangplank," she shouted as she walked ahead of me with Becky in her arms.

We reached the ship. "My husband has the boarding papers," I sighed in desperation.

"I'll carry the child onto the ship; you wait down here," she advised as she began her ascent up the gangplank.

"Marion!" I heard someone call.

"I'm here!" I screamed, and John came running towards me. "Thank goodness, you made it! I'll take the backpack. Can you fold up the stroller and take the overnighter? Please hold on tight and follow behind me," I pleaded. John hated heights and swinging bridges even more than I, but he rose to the challenge. "Look straight ahead," I yelled.

At the top of the gangplank, right at the entrance door, stood the Red Cross lady with Becky in her arms. She handed me the squirming toddler.

"Thank you ever so much," said John.

"Don't leave your family again!" the woman sternly admonished John, and then she hurried down the gangplank. The ship left at 1:32 P.M.

The best part of the voyage was the fact that we soon forgot about it. No sensible person would cross the Atlantic between October 29 and November 6 with a small child—or even alone. We encountered winds of force ten (gale) on the Beaufort Scale, where zero denotes "calm" and twelve "hurricane force." From the very first day till November 4 both John and Becky were desperately seasick. I was able to totter around trying to take care of them. The steward supplied packages of anti-seasickness suppositories and assured me that the dining room was empty. Whenever I could, I collected rolls and crackers from our table and took them to our cabin to keep my patients from starving. The day before our arrival the weather turned calm and sunny, and when we steamed into New York Harbor on November 6 we stood on deck (I was holding on to the leash of Becky's harness) and waved to the Statue of Liberty.

We docked at 1 P.M., debarked at 2 P.M., and waited around for the customs inspection until 4 P.M. The temperature in New York was seventy-four degrees, and we were melting in our heavy coats. We had forgotten that early November can be warm and sunny. Becky was completely bewildered by the chaos on the dock. She stood wide-eyed and hungry by her stroller, holding Püppi in one hand. John's parents (Grandma and Grandpa) and my parents (Oma and Opa) had come to meet us but weren't permitted on the dock until 4 P.M. Grandpa had the courage to argue with a guard.

"My little granddaughter has had nothing to eat since breakfast," he explained. The guard allowed him to give an apple to Becky and to take a picture of the new little immigrant.

We spent two days in New York City, meeting with relatives and friends who wanted to greet Becky, and trying unsuccessfully to buy some summer clothes for the family. John reclaimed his car from the garage that had stored it during our trip and loaded the four pieces of luggage and the stroller. Grandma had packed box lunches for the trip. There was enough hugging and kissing to make up for all the weeks we had been away. And then we started the journey home.

When we reached home at 6 P.M. on Saturday, November 8, 1958, we were given a heroes' welcome by our neighbors. A huge sign above the house entrance proclaimed "Hi, Becky!" Friends surprised us with a home-cooked dinner. John dragged the suitcases into the house.

"The unpacking can wait," he announced. "There won't be any traveling for a long time. Tonight we'll sleep again in our own bed, and Becky will have her own room. We are happy to be back, but we'll need time to unwind from the excitement of our successful search. But one thing we are sure of: we are home at last, all *three* of us. Our greatest adventures still lie ahead."

Epilogue

As we watched Rebecca develop, we came to realize more and more that a great deal of her character and personality was shaped before she came to us. We tried to build on that base by surrounding her with love, books, music, and art, and by taking her on trips to Europe and Israel. By the time Rebecca was sixteen, she had become an experienced actress who had starred in leading roles at the local theater club.

Rebecca continued to be the independent spirit she had been in Miss Heins's children's home, and during her adolescence occasionally got into trouble because of her anti-authoritarian attitude. Since college graduation and an additional two years of nursing school, Rebecca has built a career in nursing. Her deep compassion, knowledge, and technical skills have earned her the love of countless patients.

SOURCES

Bollgöhn, Sybille. *Jüdische Familien in Lüneburg (Jewish Families in Lüneburg)*. Lüneburg: Geschichtswerkstatt Lüneburg e.V., 1995. (German)

Dawidowicz, Lucy S. *The War Against the Jews 1933–1945*. New York: Rinehart and Winston, 1975.

Dettmering, Erhart, Herausgeber. *Zur Geschichte der Synagoge und der jüdischen Gemeinde in Marburg. (Concerning the Synagogue and Jewish Community in Marburg)*. Marburger Stadtschriften zur Geschichte und Kultur, 39. 2. Verbesserte Auflage. Marburg: 1993. (German)

Diamant, Adolf. *Zerstörte Synagogen vom November 1938: Eine Bestandsaufnahme (Synagogues that were destroyed in November 1938: An Inventory)*. Frankfurt am Main, 1978. (German)

Ettinger, Elzbieta. *Hannah Arendt/Martin Heidegger*. New Haven and London: Yale University Press, 1995.

Geschichtswerkstatt Lüneburg e.V., *Lüneburg Unter dem Haken-kreuz: Ein antifaschistischer Stadtrundgang (Lüneburg under the Swastika: An Anti-fascist Tour of the Town)*. Lüneburg, 1995. (German)

Gribetz, Judah; Greenstein, Edward L.; and Stein, Regina S. *The Timetables of Jewish History*. New York: Simon & Schuster, 1993.

Grun, Bernard. *The Timetables of History: A Horizontal Linkage of People and Events. New York: Simon & Shuster, 1979.*

Jones, Priscilla Dale. "British Policy Towards German Crimes Against German Jews, 1939-1945." *Thirty-Sixth Yearbook of the Leo Baeck Institute*. London: Secker & Warburg, 1991.

Jüdische Gräber in Giessen, hrsg. Magistrat der Universitätsstadt Giessen, 1995 (Jewish Graves in Giessen. Published by the Office of the Mayor of the University-City of Giessen, 1995). (German)

Knausz, Erwin. *Die Jüdische Bevölkerung Giessens 1933–1945*, 4. erweiterte Auflage (*The Jewish Population of Giessen 1933–1945.* 4th expanded edition) Wiesbaden: Kommission für die Geschichte der Juden in Hessen, 1987 (Commission for the History of the Jews in Hesse). (German)

Konzentrationslager Bergen-Belsen: Berichte und Dokumente. Bergen-Belsen Schriften (Concentration Camp Bergen-Belsen: Reports and Documents. Bergen-Belsen Publications). Hannover, 1995. (German)

Kralovitz, R. and B. *Giessen: Da war nachher nichts mehr da. Ein Dokumentarbericht (Giessen: Afterwards there was nothing left. A documentary report).* Giessen: 1983. (German)

Krizsan, Julius H. *Bergen-Belsen: Menschen und ihre Schicksale (Bergen-Belsen: Individuals and their Fate).* Celle: Verein zur Förderung politischer Literatur e.V., 1987 (Celle: Association for the Promotion of Political Literature, Inc.) (German)

Kurlansky, Mark. *A Chosen Few: The Resurrection of European Jewry.* Reading, Massachusetts: Addison-Wesley Publishing Co., 1995.

Laqueur, Walter. *Europe in Our Time: A History 1945–1992.* New York: Penguin Books, 1992.

Lichtenstein, Erwin. *Bericht an meine Familie: Ein Leben zwischen Danzig und Israel (Report to my Family: A Life between Danzig and Israel).* Darmstadt: Hermann Luchterhand Verlag, GmbH, Co. KG, 1985. (German)

Maor, Harry. *Über den Wiederaufbau der jüdischen Gemeinden in Deutschland seit 1945 (A study of the Reconstruction of Jewish Communities in Germany since 1945).* Mainz: Johannes Gutenberg Universität, 1961. (German)

Marx, Albert. *Geschichte der Juden in Niedersachsen (History of the Jews of Lower Saxony)*. Hannover, 1995. (German)

Rheme, Günter, and Haase, Konstantin. *...Mit Rumpf und Stumpf ausrotten...: Zur Geschichte der Juden in Marburg und Umgebung nach 1933*. (...To Destroy Root and Trunk...: Commentary on the History of the Jews of Marburg and Environs after 1933). Marburger Stadtschriften zur Geschichte und Kultur, 6. Marburg: 1982. (German)

Reilly, Jo. "No Time for Mourning: The Liberation of Bergen-Belsen Concentration Camp." *Aufbau*. April 28, 1995

Wolff, Marion F. *The Shrinking Circle: Memories of Nazi Berlin, 1933–1939*. New York: UAHC Press, 1989.